Collins

Unlocking
SPANISH
with
Paul Noble

Published by Collins
An imprint of HarperCollins Publishers
Westerhill Road
Bishopbriggs
Glasgow G64 2QT

HarperCollins Publishers
Macken House
39/40 Mayor Street Upper
Dublin 1 D01 C9W8 Ireland

First edition 2017

10 9 8 7

© Paul Noble 2017

ISBN 978-0-00-813583-6
US ISBN 978-0-00-854720-2

Collins® is a registered trademark of
HarperCollins Publishers Limited

Typeset by Davidson Publishing Solutions,
Glasgow

Printed in Italy by Grafica Veneta S.p.A.

A catalogue record for this book is available
from the British Library.

If you would like to comment on any aspect
of this book, please contact us at the given
address or online.
E-mail dictionaries@harpercollins.co.uk
www.facebook.com/collinsdictionary
@collinsdict

Acknowledgements
Images from Shutterstock.

MANAGING EDITOR
Maree Airlie

CONTRIBUTORS
Alice Grandison
Maggie Seaton
Tony Galvez

FOR THE PUBLISHER
Gerry Breslin
Holly Tarbet
Kevin Robbins
Vaila Donnachie

People who know no Spanish at all

People who know some Spanish already

People who studied Spanish at school

People who didn't study Spanish at school

People who didn't like how languages were taught at school

People who are amazed by just how closely grammar
books resemble furniture assembly instructions

Who is this book for?

People who think they can't learn a foreign language

People who've listened to one of Paul Noble's audio courses

People who haven't listened to one of Paul Noble's audio courses

People learning Spanish for the first time

People coming back to the language after a break

People curious about whether they can learn a language

People who feel confused by the way languages
are normally taught

Contents

Did you know you
already speak Spanish?

Did you know you already speak Spanish?

Did you know you already speak Spanish? That you speak it every day? That you read and write it every day? That you use it with your friends, with your family, at work, down the post office – even in the shower when you read the label on the shampoo bottle?

Were you aware of that fact?

Well, even if you weren't, it's nevertheless true.

Of course, you might not have realised at the time that what you were reading / saying / writing was actually Spanish but I can prove to you that it was. Just take a look at these Spanish words below but, as you do so, use your thumb to cover the letter at the end of each word:

importante	romántico	urgente	sarcasmo
artista	tímido	racismo	novela
dentista	accidente	rápido	optimismo

fantástico	elegante	válido	público
lista	cliente	pánico	inteligente
terrorismo			

As your thumb has hopefully helped you to realise, these are words that exist not only in Spanish but also in English. And, in fact, these are by no means isolated examples of words that exist in both Spanish and English but rather they are merely the tip of a *truly enormous* iceberg.

In fact, around half of all English words have close equivalents in Spanish. Yes, that's right, ***half!***

If we begin using these words, together with an extremely subtle method that shows you how to put them into sentences in a way that's almost effortless, then becoming a competent Spanish speaker becomes really quite easy.

The only thing that *you* will need to do to make this happen is to follow the three simple rules printed on the following pages. These rules will explain to you how to use this book so that you can begin unlocking the Spanish language for yourself in a matter of hours.

Well, what are you waiting for?
Turn the page!

Rule Number 1:
Don't skip anything!

Using this book is extremely simple – and highly effective – *if* you follow its three simple rules.

If you don't want to follow them, then I recommend that, instead of reading the book, you use it to prop up a wobbly coffee table, as it won't work if you don't follow the rules. Now get ready – because here's the first one!

Each and every little thing in this book has been put where it is, in a very particular order, for a very particular reason. So, if the book asks you to read or do something, then do it! Who's the teacher after all, you or me, eh?

Also, each part of the book builds on and reinforces what came before it. If you start skipping sections, you will end up confused and lost. Instead, you should just take your time and gently work your way through the book at your own pace – *but without skipping anything!*

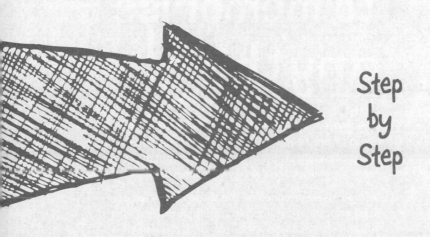

Step
by
Step

Rule Number 2:
Don't try to memorise anything!

Trying to jam things into your head is boring *and* it doesn't work. People often cram for tests and then forget everything the moment they walk out of the exam. Clearly, we don't want that happening here.

Instead, I have designed this book so that any word or idea taught in it will come up multiple times. You don't need to worry about trying to remember or memorise anything because the necessary repetition is actually already built in. In fact, trying to memorise what you're learning is likely to hinder rather than help your progress.

So, just work your way through the book in a relaxed way and, if you happen to forget something, don't worry because, as I say, you will be reminded of it again, multiple times, later on.

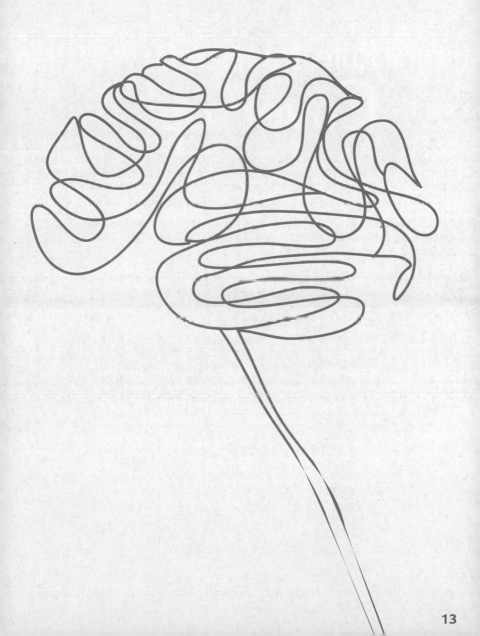

Rule Number 3:
Cover up!

No, I'm not being a puritan grandmother and telling you to put on a long-sleeved cardigan. Instead, I'm asking you to take a bookmark or piece of paper and use it to cover up any **orange text** that you come across as you work your way through the book.

These **orange bits** are the answers to the various riddles, challenges and questions that I will pose as I lead you into the Spanish language. If you read these answers without at least trying to work out the solutions first, then the book simply won't work for you.

So, make sure to use something to cover up the bits of **orange text** in the book while you have a go at trying to work out the answers. It doesn't matter if you sometimes get them wrong because it is by trying to think out the answers that you will learn how to use the language.

Trust me on this, you will see that it works from the very next page of this book.

Take a look at the page on the right to see how to use your bookmark or piece of paper to cover up correctly.

How about "I spent"?

Pasé
(pass-ay)

"I reserved" / "I booked"?

Reservé
(re-surv-ay)

I prepared /

Preparé
(pre-par-ay)

"I ordered"?

Ordené
(or-den-ay)

"I paid" in Spanish is:

Pagué
(pag-ay)

"The bill" in Spanish is literally "the addition", which in Spanish is:

la cuenta
(la kwen-ta)

So how would you say "I paid the bill"?

Pagué la cuenta.
(pag-ay la kwen-ta)

Again, how would you say "I booked a table"?

Reservé una mesa.
(re-surv-ay oon-er may-ser)

What about "I ordered dinner"?

Ordené la cena.
(or-den-ay la say-ner / thay-ner)

And again what was "I paid the bill"?

Pagué la cuenta.
(pag-ay la kwen-ta)

Let's now try making a list out of these things. We'll start by saying "I booked a table, ordered dinner, paid the bill." Take your time working it out in your head, bit by bit - there really is no rush! So again "I booked a table, ordered dinner, paid the bill":

> Make sure to cover up any orange words, just like this!

luego pagué la cuenta
(loo-way-go pag-ay la kwen-ta)

And what was "and" in Spanish?

y
(ee)

So now say "and then paid the bill".

y luego pagué la cuenta
(ee loo-way-go pag-ay la kwen-ta)

Okay, let's try to put this all together and say "I booked a table, ordered dinner and then paid the bill."

Reservé una mesa, ordené la cena y luego pagué la cuenta.
(re-surv-ay oon-er may-ser, or-den-ay la say-ner / thay-ner ee loo-way-go pag-ay la kwen-ta)

Not a bad sentence. Let's make it bigger still.

How about "I spent"?

Pasé
(pass-ay)

"I reserved" / "I booked"?

Reservé
(re-surv-ay)

"I prepared"?

Preparé
(pre-par-ay)

"I ordered"?

Ordené
(or-den-ay)

"I paid" in Spanish is:

Pagué
(pag-ay)

"The bill" in Spanish is literally "the addition", which in Spanish is:

la cuenta
(la kwen-ta)

So how would you say "I paid the bill"?

Pagué la cuenta.
(pag-ay la kwen-ta)

Again, how would you say "I booked a table"?

Reservé una mesa.
(re-surv-ay oon-er may-ser)

What about "I ordered dinner"?

Ordené la cena.
(or-den-ay la say-ner / thay-ner)

And again what was "I paid the bill"?

Pagué la cuenta.
(pag-ay la kwen-ta)

Let's now try making a list out of these things. We'll start by saying "I booked a table, ordered dinner, paid the bill." Take your time working it out in your head, bit by bit - there really is no rush! So again "I booked a table, ordered dinner, paid the bill":

Reservé una mesa, ordené la cena, pagué la cuenta.
(re-surv-ay oon-er may-ser, or-den-ay la say-ner / thay-ner, pag-ay la kwen-ta)

Let's add "then" into this sentence to make it sound more natural. "Then" in

> Then, having tried to work out the answer, uncover and check!

And what was "and" in Spanish?

y
(ee)

So now say "and then paid the bill".

y luego pagué la cuenta
(ee loo-way-go pag-ay la kwen-ta)

Okay, let's try to put this all together and say "I booked a table, ordered dinner and then paid the bill."

Reservé una mesa, ordené la cena y luego pagué la cuenta.
(re-surv-ay oon-er may-ser, or-den-ay la say-ner / thay-ner ee loo-way-go pag-ay la kwen-ta)

Not a bad sentence. Let's make it bigger still.

42

43

CHAPTER 1

I spent the
weekend in
Barcelona...
and it
was lovely.

> "I spent the weekend in Barcelona... and it was lovely."
> Not such a complicated sentence in English, is it?
> Or is it...?

I have taught many people over the years, ranging from those who know no Spanish at all through to those who may have studied Spanish for several years at school, and yet whether they have studied the language before or not, almost none of them tend to be able to construct a basic sentence like this when I first meet them.

Admittedly, they might know how to say other far less useful things, like "I'm 37 years old and have two sisters and a goldfish" – an unusual conversation opener from my perspective – but they nevertheless can't say what they did at the weekend.

Well, in just a few minutes' time, you *will* be able to do this – even if you've never learnt any Spanish before.

Just remember though: **don't skip anything,** *don't* **waste your time trying to memorise anything but** *do* **use your bookmark to cover up anything orange you find on each page.**

Okay now, let's begin!

To say "I visited" in Spanish, you simply take the English word "visit" and add "é" (pronounced "ay") onto the end of it.

So, do this now, take "visit" and add "é" (pronounced "ay") onto the end of it. What does that give you?

Visité
(pronounced "visit-ay")

> Did you remember to cover up the orange words while you worked out the answer?

And this simply means "I visited".

"Madrid" in Spanish is, of course:

Madrid
(pronounced "ma-drid")

18

So, given what you have been taught so far, how do you think you would say "I visited Madrid"?

Visité Madrid.
(visit-ay ma-drid)

And how do you think you would say "I visited Barcelona"?

Visité Barcelona.
(visit ay bar sair loan or / bar thair loan or [1])

So far you have created the word for "I visited" in Spanish simply by taking the English word "visit" and adding "é" (pronounced "ay") onto the end of it.

You can now do something similar with the English word "pass".

Just as before, what I want you to do is to take the English word "pass" and simply add "é" (pronounced "ay") onto the end of it.

Do that now – what do you get?

Pasé
(pass-ay)

---

1   Have you noticed that there are two pronunciation suggestions for Barcelona given below the word? Why is that? Well, it's because a letter "c" in front of an "e" in Spanish is pronounced like an "s" in Latin America but like a "th" (as in "**th**ink") in most of Spain.

This makes "Barcelona" in Latin America sound very similar to how it does in English, whereas in Spain it sounds as if the speaker has a lisp, making Barcelona sound more like "bar-thair-loan-er". You should choose whichever pronunciation you prefer.

This means "I passed" (and also "I spent" (time)).

And oh yes, oops, you'll have noticed that we lost an "s" in the process of doing this – oh well, never mind, what's a letter between friends, eh?!

So again, tell me, what is "I passed" (and also "I spent") in Spanish?

Pasé
(pass-ay)

"August" in Spanish is:

agosto
(a-gost-oh)

So how would you say "I spent August" (literally "I passed August")?

Pasé agosto
(pass-ay a-gost-oh)

"In Barcelona" in Spanish is:

en Barcelona
(en bar-sair-loan-er / bar-thair-loan-er)

So how would you say "I spent August in Barcelona"?

Pasé agosto en Barcelona.
(pass-ay a-gost-oh en bar-sair-loan-er / bar-thair-loan-er)

How about "I spent August in Madrid"?

Pasé agosto en Madrid.
(pass-ay a-gost-oh en ma-drid)

"The weekend" in Spanish is literally "the end of week", which is:

el fin de semana
(el fin dey sem-arn-er)

So how would you say "I spent the weekend in Madrid" (literally "I passed the end of week in Madrid")?

Pasé el fin de semana en Madrid.
(pass-ay el fin dey sem-arn-er en ma-drid)

How about "I spent the weekend in Barcelona"?

Pasé el fin de semana en Barcelona.
(pass-ay el fin dey sem-arn-er en bar-sair-loan-er / bar-thair-loan-er)

•Time to steal some words!
Word Robbery Number 1

Let's forget our weekend in Barcelona for just one moment now and start stealing some words. Around half the words in modern English have come into our language via Latin languages, such as Spanish. Once you can identify them, you will have a large, instant, usable vocabulary in Spanish. And after all, why bother learning Spanish vocabulary when you can simply steal it!

The first group of words we are going to steal are words that end in "**ic**" and "**ical**" in English.

Words like "romant**ic**", "exot**ic**", "illog**ical**", "typ**ical**" and so on.

There are around 750 of these in English and they are largely similar in Spanish, except that in Spanish they end in "**ico**" (pronounced "ick-oh"), becoming "román**tico**", "exó**tico**", "iló**gico**", "típ**ico**" and so on.

Let's now see how we can work these into our weekend in Barcelona and expand our range of expressions in Spanish!

Words stolen so far 750

Bearing in mind what we've just learnt in the Word Robbery above, let's try changing the "**ic**" on the end of the English word "romant**ic**" into "**ico**".

Doing this, what will "romantic" be in Spanish?

romántico
(roe-man-tick-oh)

And so what would "exotic" be in Spanish?

exótico
(ex-ot-ick-oh)

Let's now try doing the same with "ical". Change the "ical" on the end of "typical" into "ico".

Doing this, what will "typical" be in Spanish?

típico[2]
(tip-ick-oh)

And what will "political" be?

político
(po-li-tick-oh)

Let's now try using these "ico" words to expand our range of expressions and to make some more complex sentences in Spanish.

"It was" in Spanish is:

Fue
(fway)

So, how would you say "it was political"?

Fue político.
(fway po-li-tick-oh)

And how would you say "it was typical"?

Fue típico.
(fway tip-ick-oh)

---

2   You'll sometimes notice additional spelling changes when you carry out these Word Robberies, such as the
     way the "y" in "typical" becomes an "i" in Spanish. Please don't worry about this though! It doesn't affect the
     pronunciation and you'll pick up any spelling differences as you go along and as you get used to seeing the
     words written in Spanish.

How about "it was exotic"?

Fue exótico.
(fway ex-ot-ick-oh)

And how do you think you would say "it was romantic"?

Fue romántico.
(fway roe-man-tick-oh)

To say something is "lovely" in Spanish, you will say it is "adorable".
"Adorable" in Spanish is:

adorable
(ad-or-arb-lay)

So, how would you say "It was lovely" / "It was adorable"?

Fue adorable.
(fway ad-or-arb-lay)

Do you remember how to say "I visited" in Spanish?

Visité
(visit-ay)

And do you remember how to say "I spent" (literally "I passed")?

Pasé
(pass-ay)

So how would you say "I spent August"?

Pasé agosto
(pass-ay a-gost-oh)

And what is "in Barcelona" in Spanish?

en Barcelona
(en bar-sair-loan-er / bar-thair-loan-er)

So how would you say "I spent August in Barcelona"?

Pasé agosto en Barcelona.
(pass-ay a-gost-oh en bar-sair-loan-er / bar-thair-loan-er)

What was "the weekend" (literally "the end of week") in Spanish?

el fin de semana
(el fin dey sem-arn-er)

So how would you say "I spent the weekend in Barcelona"?

Pasé el fin de semana en Barcelona.
(pass-ay el fin dey sem-arn-er en bar-sair-loan-er / bar-thair-loan-er)

Now again, what was "lovely" in Spanish?

adorable
(ad-or-arb-lay)

And do you remember how to say "it was"?

fue
(fway)

So how would you say "it was lovely"?

Fue adorable.
(fway ad-or-arb-lay)

The word for "and" in Spanish is:

y
(ee)

So, how would you say "...and it was lovely"?

...y fue adorable
(ee fway ad-or-arb-lay)

Now, putting what you've learnt together, say "I spent the weekend in Barcelona...
and it was lovely." Take your time to work this out, bit by bit, there's no rush!

Pasé el fin de semana en Barcelona... y fue adorable.
(pass-ay el fin dey sem-arn-er en bar-sair-loan-er / bar-thair-loan-er... ee
fway ad-or-arb-lay)

So, you can now construct the sentence with which we started the chapter – and,
as you will soon discover, this is just the very beginning of your journey into Spanish!

You just learnt how to say (amongst other things) "I spent the weekend in Barcelona... and it was lovely".

Having done this, we are now going to move on to expanding what you can say through the use of additional "building blocks".

The new building blocks you are going to learn will allow you to begin instantly expanding your range of expressions in the Spanish language.

So far, some of the building blocks you have already learnt include:

You already know how to use these building blocks to construct a sentence. So, once again, how would you say "I spent the weekend in Barcelona"?

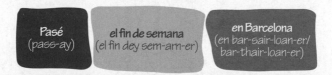

As you can see, you already know how to build the three building blocks above into a sentence. Take a look now at six new building blocks below. Just have a glance over them and then I'll show you how we're going to add these into the mix of what we've learnt so far.

Pasamos
(pass-arm-oss)
We spent

Pasó
(pass-o)
You spent

en España
(en es-pan-ya)
in Spain

la Navidad
(la na-vee-dadd)
Christmas*

septiembre
(sep-Lee-em-bray)
September

en México
(en me-hee-koe)
in Mexico

*literally "the Christmas"

So, here we have six new building blocks to play with.

Now, first things first: please don't to try to memorise them. No, no, no! Instead, I simply want you to play with your building blocks. After all, that's what building blocks are for, isn't it?

The way you're going to play with them is like this: on the next page, they have been put in three piles and all I want you to do is to make sentences with them. You'll do this by each time using one building block from the first pile, one from the second, and one from the third.

You will find that you can say a lot of different things using them in this way and it's up to you what sentences you make. The only thing I want you to make sure you do is to use every building block at least once. Also, please don't bother writing down the sentences you make. Instead, say them out loud, or, if you're not in a place where you can do this, say them in your head. Now, off you go; make as many sentences as you can!

1

Pasé
(pass-ay)
I spent

Pasó
(pass-o)
You spent

Pasamos
(pass-arm-oss)
We spent

2

el fin de semana
(el fin dey sem-arn-er)
the weekend

septiembre
(sep-tee-em-bray)
September

la Navidad[3]
(la na-vee-dadd)
Christmas

3

en Barcelona
(en bar-sair-loan-er/
bar-thair-loan-er)
in Barcelona

en España
(en es-pan-ya)
in Spain

en México
(en me-hee-koe)
in Mexico

---

3   In Spanish words such as "Navidad" or "Madrid", which end in the letter "d", you'll notice when you hear native speakers pronounce them that the "d" is pronounced very, very softly. So, when you say "Navidad" or "Madrid" or any Spanish word ending in a "d", try to just touch the "d" at the end of the word very lightly – doing so will help your Spanish sound much more authentic.

The Checklist

You have now reached the final part of Chapter 1. Once you have finished this short section, you will not only have completed your first chapter but you will also understand how this book works as the other chapters follow the same pattern, with your Spanish getting ever more sophisticated as you complete each chapter.

The section you are now on will be the final part of each chapter and is what I call "The Checklist". It involves nothing more than a read-through of a selection of some of the words or expressions you have so far encountered.

You will actually see The Checklist twice. The first time you will see that the Spanish words are written in **black** (on the left-hand side) and that the English words are written in orange (on the right-hand side) – and you know what orange means... cover up!

So, what I want you to do here is to cover up the English words (which are written in orange on the right-hand side) while you read through the list of Spanish words on the left. Read through them all, from the top of the list to the bottom, and see if you can recall what they mean in English (uncover one orange word at a time to check if you've remembered the meaning correctly). If you can go through the entire list, giving the correct English meaning for each of the Spanish words / expressions **without making more than three mistakes in total**, then you're done. If not, then go through the list again. Keep doing this, either working from the top of the list to the bottom or from the bottom to the top (it doesn't matter which) until you can do it **without making more than three mistakes**.

Got it? Then let's go!

el fin de semana (el fin day sem-arn-er)	the weekend
romántico (roe-man-tick-oh)	romantic
típico (tip-ick-oh)	typical
político (po-li-tick-oh)	political
lógico (lo-hee-koh)	logical
histórico (ee-sto-rick-oh)	historical
crítico (kri-tick-oh)	critical
clásico (clas-ick-oh)	classical
eléctrico (el-ek-trick-oh)	electrical

idéntico (ee-dent-ick-oh)	identical
biológico (bee-oh-lo-hee-koh)	biological
Visité (visit-ay)	I visited
Barcelona (bar-sair-loan-er / bar-thair-loan-er)	Barcelona
Madrid (ma-drid)	Madrid
Visité Madrid. (visit-ay ma-drid)	I visited Madrid.
Pasé (pass-ay)	I spent
Pasó (pass-o)	You spent
Pasamos (pass-arm-oss)	We spent
septiembre (sep-tee-em-brey)	September
la Navidad (la na-vee-dad)	Christmas (literally "the Christmas")
en Barcelona (en bar-sair-loan-er / bar-thair-loan-er)	in Barcelona
en España (en es-pan-ya)	in Spain
en México (en me-hee-koe)	in Mexico
Pasamos la Navidad en México. (pass-arm-oss la na-vee-dad en me-hee-koe)	We spent Christmas in Mexico.
Pasó septiembre en España. (pass-o sep-tee-em-brey en es-pan-ya)	You spent September in Spain.
y (ee)	and
fue (fway)	it was
fue romántico (fway roe-man-tick-oh)	it was romantic
adorable (ad-or-arb-lay)	lovely / adorable
fue adorable (fway ad-or-arb-lay)	it was lovely / it was adorable
Pasé el fin de semana en Barcelona... y fue adorable. (pass-ay el fin dey sem-arn-er en bar-sair-loan-er / bar-thair-loan-er ee fway ad-or-arb-lay)	I spent the weekend in Barcelona... and it was lovely.

Finished working through that checklist and made less than three mistakes? Yes? Wonderful!

As that's the case, what I want you to do now is to repeat exactly the same process again below, except that this time you'll be reading through the *English* and trying to recall the Spanish. So, it will be the other way around. So, just relax and work your way up and down the list until you can give the correct Spanish translation for each of the *English* words / expressions **again without making more than three mistakes in total**. It's not a competition – and I'm not asking you to memorise them.

Just look at the English words (on the left-hand side) while you cover up the orange Spanish words on the right-hand side and see if you can remember how to say them in Spanish. You'll be surprised by how much you get right, even on the first try.

Okay, off you go!

the weekend	el fin de semana (el fin dey sem-arn-er)
romantic	romántico (roe-man-tick-oh)
typical	típico (tip-ick-oh)
political	político (po-li-tick-oh)
logical	lógico (lo-hee-koh)
historical	histórico (ee-sto-rick-oh)
critical	crítico (kri-tick-oh)
classical	clásico (clas-ick-oh)
electrical	eléctrico (el-ek-trick-oh)
identical	idéntico (ee-dent-ick-oh)
biological	biológico (bee-oh-lo-hee-koh)
I visited	Visité (visit-ay)
Barcelona	Barcelona (bar-sair-loan-er / bar-thair-loan-er)
Madrid	Madrid (ma-drid)
I visited Madrid.	Visité Madrid. (visit-ay ma-drid)
I spent	Pasé (pass-ay)

31

You spent	Pasó (pass-o)
We spent	Pasamos (pass-arm-oss)
September	septiembre (sep-tee-em-brey)
Christmas	la Navidad (la na-vee-dad)
in Barcelona	en Barcelona (en bar-sair-loan-er / bar-thair-loan-er)
in Spain	en España (en es-pan-ya)
in Mexico	en México (en me-hee-koe)
We spent Christmas in Mexico.	Pasamos la Navidad en México. (pass-arm-oss la na-vee-dad en me-hee-koe)
You spent September in Spain.	Pasó septiembre en España. (pass-o sep-tee-em-brey en es-pan-ya)
and	y (ee)
it was	fue (fway)
it was romantic	fue romántico (fway roe-man-tick-oh)
lovely / adorable	adorable (ad-or-arb-lay)
it was lovely / it was adorable	fue adorable (fway ad-or-arb-lay)
I spent the weekend in Barcelona... and it was lovely.	Pasé el fin de semana en Barcelona... y fue adorable. (pass-ay el fin dey sem-arn-er en bar-sair-loan-er / bar-thair-loan-er ee fway ad-or-arb-lay)

Well, that's it, you're done with Chapter 1! Now, don't try to hold onto or remember anything you've learnt here. Everything you learn in earlier chapters will be brought up again and reinforced in later chapters. You don't need to do anything extra or make any effort to memorise anything. The book has been organised so that it does that for you. Now, off you go and have a rest. You've earned it!

Between Chapters Tip!

Between chapters, I'm going to be giving you various tips on language learning. These will range from useful tips about the Spanish language itself to advice on how to fit learning a language in with your daily routine. Ready for the first one? Here it is!

Tip Number One – study (at least a little) every day!

Learning a language is like building a fire – if you don't tend to it, it will go out. So, once you have decided to learn a foreign language, you really should study it every day.

It doesn't have to be for a long time though. Just five or ten minutes each day will be enough, so long as you keep it up. Doing these five or ten minutes will stop you forgetting what you've already learnt and, over time, will let you put more meat on the bones of what you're learning.

As for what counts towards those five or ten minutes, well that's up to you. Whilst you're working with this book, I would recommend that your five or ten minutes should be spent here learning with me. Once you're done here, however, your five or ten minutes could be spent reading a Spanish newspaper, watching a Spanish film, or chatting with a Spanish-speaking acquaintance. You could even attend a class if you want to learn in a more formal setting. The important thing, though, is to make sure that you do a little every day.

CHAPTER 2

I booked a table, ordered dinner
and then paid the bill.
What did you do?

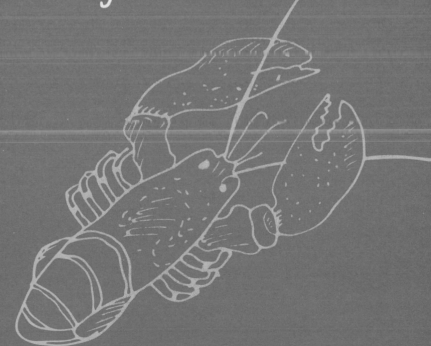

> I booked a table, ordered dinner and then paid the bill. What did you do?

The first chapter has shown you that you can learn how to create full and complex sentences in Spanish with relative ease. It also began to show you how you can convert huge numbers of English words into Spanish and then start using them straight away.

We will be doing more of both here, which will allow you to make enormous strides with your Spanish in an incredibly short space of time.

Let's begin by carrying out a second Word Robbery...

- Time to steal some words!
'Word Robbery Number 2

The second group of words we are going to steal are words that end in "ion" and "ation". Words that end in "ation" in English usually end in "ación" in Spanish. Take a look:

Words such as:

decoration	decoración	invitation	invitación
cooperation	cooperación	association	asociación
imagination	imaginación	innovation	innovación
preparation	preparación	irritation	irritación
reservation	reservación		

There are more than 1250 "ion" words in English and they are related to similar words in Spanish, as you can see above; we can start using these in Spanish right now.

Adding them to the words we've already stolen so far, we have now reached a total of 2000 words stolen – and we're only on Chapter 2!

Words stolen so far 2000

So, we've carried out our second Word Robbery and have gained more than 1000 words ending in "ion" and "ation" and it only took us 30 seconds to "learn" them.

Now, words ending in "ation" in English actually come with yet another benefit. Not only can we steal them to use in Spanish in the way shown above, but we can also use them to make the past tense in Spanish.

Let me show you how.

We'll take "reservación" (reservation) as an example.

The first thing we're going to do with "reservación" is to cut off the "ación" at the end. Do this now – what are you left with?

reserv
(re-surv)

Good. Now, onto the end of this, I want you to add "é" (pronounced "ay").

Doing so, what does that give you?

reservé
(re-surv-ay)

This means "I reserved".

So, by simply adding the letter "é" (pronounced "ay" – just like it is on the end of the English word "café") we have accessed the past tense in Spanish.

Now, let's try doing this again, this time with the word "invitación". Once more, cut off the "ación" from the end of the word and replace it with the "é" you find at the end of the word "café".

What do you get?

invité
(in-vit-ay)

This means "I invited".

Let's try this one more time, as the more practice you get, the easier it will become.

We'll take the word "preparación" as our starting point this time. Again, cut off the "ación" from the end and add an "é" in its place.

What does that give you?

preparé
(pre-par-ay)

This means "I prepared".

"The dinner" in Spanish is:

la cena
(la say-ner / thay-ner)

So, how would you say "I prepared the dinner"?

Preparé la cena.
(pre-par-ay la say-ner / thay-ner)

Alright, let's return again to our 1250 "ation" words for a moment.

Once more, what was "reservation" in Spanish?

reservación
(re-surv-ass-ee-on / re-surv-ath-ee-on)

Now, as before, let's cut the "ación" off the end of "reservación" and replace it with the "é" from "café" to create the word that means "reserved" in Spanish.

So, doing that, what is "reserved"?

reservé
(re-surv-ay)

And this actually means both "reserved" and "booked". So, how would you say, "I reserved" / "I booked"?

Reservé
(re-surv-ay)

"A table" in Spanish is:

una mesa
(oon-er may-ser)

So, how would you say "I reserved a table" / "I booked a table"?

Reservé una mesa.
(re-surv-ay oon-er may-ser)

"For you" in Spanish is:

para usted
(pa-ra oo-stedd)

So, how would you say "I reserved a table for you" / "I booked a table for you"?

Reservé una mesa para usted.
(re-surv-ay oon-er may-ser pa-ra oo-stedd)

And again, what was "the dinner" in Spanish?

la cena
(la say-ner / thay-ner)

And what was "for you"?

para usted
(pa-ra oo-stedd)

So, if "para usted" means "for you", what do you think is the word for "for" in Spanish?

para
(pa-ra)

Now, to say "for dinner" in Spanish, you will literally say "for *the* dinner". How do you think you would say that?

para la cena
(pa-ra la say-ner / thay-ner)

And so how would you say "I reserved a table for dinner" / "I booked a table for dinner"?

Reservé una mesa para la cena.
(re-surv-ay oon-er may-ser pa-ra la say-ner / thay-ner)

As you can see, these "ation" / "ación" words really are very useful. Not only do you get more than 1000 words right away – like "reservation" (reservación), "preparation" (preparación), "information" (información), and so on – for free but these "ation" words also give you access to the past tense in Spanish, allowing you to create many, many new words such as "reserved", "prepared", "informed", and so on. And we achieve this simply by cutting off the "ation" / "ación" from the end of the word and adding an "é" in its place.

We can even create new words in some quite unexpected ways using this technique.

For instance, "ordination" in Spanish is:

ordenación
(or-den-ass-ee-on / or-den-ath-ee-on)

And so, cutting off the "ación" and replacing it with the "é" from "café", what would "I ordained" be in Spanish?

Ordené
(or-den-ay)

Now, you are probably asking yourself "why on earth am I being taught the words for 'ordination' and 'I ordained'?"

Well, the word "ordination" / "ordenación" actually refers to "the granting of holy orders" and, even more literally, means something simpler still like "ordering".

When you cut off the "ación" from the end of "ordenación" and add the "é" from "café" in its place, you end up with the Spanish word that means not only "I ordained" but also "I ordered".

So, now that you know this, how could you say in Spanish "I ordered dinner"?

Ordonó la cona.
(or-den-ay la say-ner / thay-ner)

"Soup" in Spanish is:

sopa
(soap-er)

So how would you say "I ordered soup"?

Ordené sopa.
(or-den-ay soap-er)

And once again how would you say "for dinner" (literally "for the dinner") in Spanish?

para la cena
(pa-ra la say-ner / thay-ner)

Now put these two things together and say "I ordered soup for dinner".

Ordené sopa para la cena.
(or-den-ay soap-er pa-ra la say-ner / thay-ner)

And how would you say "I ordered soup for you"?

Ordené sopa para usted.
(or-den-ay soap-er pa-ra oo-stedd)

Good, now can you recall how to say "I visited"?

Visité
(visit-ay)

How about "I spent"?

Pasé
(pass-ay)

"I reserved" / "I booked"?

Reservé
(re-surv-ay)

"I prepared"?

Preparé
(pre-par-ay)

"I ordered"?

Ordené
(or-den-ay)

"I paid" in Spanish is:

Pagué
(pag-ay)

"The bill" in Spanish is literally "the addition", which in Spanish is:

la cuenta
(la kwen-ta)

So how would you say "I paid the bill"?

Pagué la cuenta.
(pag-ay la kwen-ta)

Again, how would you say "I booked a table"?

Reservé una mesa.
(re-surv-ay oon-er may-ser)

What about "I ordered dinner"?

Ordené la cena.
(or-den-ay la say-ner / thay-ner)

And again what was "I paid the bill"?

Pagué la cuenta.
(pag-ay la kwen-ta)

Let's now try making a list out of these things. We'll start by saying "I booked a table, ordered dinner, paid the bill." Take your time working it out in your head, bit by bit – there really is no rush! So again "I booked a table, ordered dinner, paid the bill":

Reservé una mesa, ordené la cena, pagué la cuenta.
(re-surv-ay oon-er may-ser, or-den-ay la say-ner / thay-ner, pag-ay la kwen-ta)

Let's add "then" into this sentence to make it sound more natural. "Then" in Spanish is:

luego
(loo-way-go)

First try simply saying "then paid the bill". How would you say that?

luego pagué la cuenta
(loo-way-go pag-ay la kwen-ta)

And what was "and" in Spanish?

y
(ee)

So now say "and then paid the bill".

y luego pagué la cuenta
(ee loo-way-go pag-ay la kwen-ta)

Okay, let's try to put this all together and say "I booked a table, ordered dinner and then paid the bill."

Reservé una mesa, ordené la cena y luego pagué la cuenta.
(re-surv-ay oon-er may-ser, or-den-ay la say-ner / thay-ner ee loo-way-go pag-ay la kwen-ta)

Not a bad sentence. Let's make it bigger still.

Again, what is "I spent"?

Pasé
(pass-ay)

And do you remember what "you spent" is, from the "Building Blocks" section in Chapter 1?

Pasó
(pass-o)

So, as you can see, when you want to say "I..." did something in the past you add "é" onto the end of the word but when you want to say "you..." did something in the past you instead add this "ó" which we can see on the end of "you spent" above – pasó. Now, how do you say "I prepared" in Spanish?

Preparé
(pre-par-ay)

So, how do you think would you say "you prepared"?

Preparó
(pre-par-o)

So, just as with "you spent", there is this "ó" on the end, whereas when you say "I spent", "I prepared", and so on, there will be an "é" on the end.

To remember which way around these work, simply think to yourself "I need an 'é' when I talk about 'mé' in the past, but an 'ó' when I talk about 'yóu'".

Now, if you want to say "what did you prepare?" in Spanish, it's very simple. All you need to say is "what you prepared?".

"What" in Spanish is:

Qué
(kay)

Now again, how would you say "I prepared" in Spanish?

Preparé
(pre-par-ay)

44

And what about "you prepared"?

Preparó
(pre-par-o)

And how would you say "What"?

Qué
(kay)

So, how would you say "what did you prepare?" (literally "what you prepared?")?

¿Qué preparó?[4]
(kay pre-par-o)

And what is "I reserved" / "I booked" in Spanish?

Reservé
(re-surv-ay)

So how would you say "you reserved" / "you booked"?

Reservó
(re-surv-o)

So how would you say "what did you reserve?" (literally "what you reserved?")?

¿Qué reservó?
(kay re-surv-o)

Now, you'll have noticed that, when I've taught you things like "you reserved", "you prepared", "you spent", and so on, there are two words in English but in Spanish I've only given you one. You may even have wondered to yourself "where's the 'you'?".

Well, in Spanish, there is a separate word for "you" that you could add to these sentences if you wanted to but you don't normally need to. This is because, in Spanish, "reservó" by itself means "you reserved" and "preparó" by itself means "you prepared" and "pasó" by itself means "you spent". Each of these words has an "ó" on the end of them, so you know that the person means "you".

---

4   Notice how Spanish likes to use two question marks. One is placed upside down at the front while the other one goes at the end, normal way up, just like in English.

However, sometimes in Spanish you may wish to emphasise the word "you" more strongly. Perhaps, for example, you are moaning at someone about something they have done and want to say "*you* did this" or "it was *you* who prepared the dinner – and it's terrible".

At these times, when you want to really emphasise the word "you", then you should include the word itself.

So, first of all, how have we so far learnt to say "you reserved" in Spanish?

Reservó
(re-surv-o)

If you don't want to place any special, strong emphasis on the word "you", this is the way you will normally say "you reserved" in Spanish.

However, if we want to add more emphasis, we can add the word that means "you" into the sentence.

The word for "you" in Spanish is:

usted
(oo-sted)

So, now try saying "*you* reserved":

Usted reservó
(oo-sted re-surv-o)

So, the meaning is still essentially the same but there is a stronger emphasis on the word "*you*".

How would you say, again with emphasis, "*you* spent"?

Usted pasó
(oo-sted pass-o)

What about "*you* prepared"?

Usted preparó
(oo-sted pre-par-o)

If you want to turn this into a question and say "did *you* prepare?", then all you need to do is reverse the word order and say literally "prepared you?".

Do that now:

¿Preparó usted?
(pre-par-o oo-sted)

Again, how would you say "what" in Spanish?

¿Qué?
(kay)

If you want to ask "what did *you* prepare?" you will simply say "what prepared you?"
How would you say that?

¿Qué preparó usted?
(kay pre-par-o oo-sted)

"You did" in Spanish is

hizo
(ee-soe / ee-thoe)

So, how would you add more emphasis to this and say "*you* did"?

Usted hizo
(oo-sted ee-soe / ee-thoe)

Turn this into a question now and ask "did you do?" (literally "did you?"):

¿Hizo usted?
(ee-soe / ee-thoe oo-sted)

How would you say "what did you do?" (literally "what did you?")?

¿Qué hizo usted?
(kay ee-soe / ee-thoe oo-sted)

And once more, how would you say "I reserved a table" / "I booked a table"?

Reservé una mesa.
(re-surv-ay oon-er may-ser)

And how would you say "I ordered dinner"?

Ordené la cena.
(or-den-ay la say-ner / thay-ner)

And remind me, what was the word for "then" in Spanish?

luego
(loo-way-go)

And the word for "and"?

y
(ee)

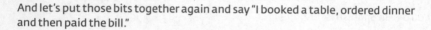

So, now say "and then paid the bill".

y luego pagué la cuenta
(ee loo-way-go pag-ay la kwen-ta)

And let's put those bits together again and say "I booked a table, ordered dinner and then paid the bill."

Reservé una mesa, ordené la cena y luego pagué la cuenta.
(re-surv-ay oon-er may-ser, or-den-ay la say-ner / thay-ner ee loo-way-go pag-ay la kwen-ta)

And let's add the final bit onto it all. Again, how would you say "What?"

¿Qué?
(kay)

And how would you say "What did *you* do?" (literally "what did you?")?

¿Qué hizo usted?
(kay ee-soe / ee-thoe oo-sted)

Now let's combine absolutely everything together and (taking your time to think it out) say "I booked a table, ordered dinner and then paid the bill. What did *you* do?"

Reservé una mesa, ordené la cena y luego pagué la cuenta. ¿Qué hizo usted?
(re-surv-ay oon-er may-ser, or-den-ay la say-ner / thay-ner, ee loo-way-go pag-ay la kwen-ta. kay ee-soe / ee-thoe oo-sted)

How did you find that final, complex sentence? Try it a few more times, even if you've got it right, until you feel comfortable constructing it. Every time you practise building these long sentences, the naturalness and fluidity of your spoken Spanish will improve and your confidence in speaking the language will rise along with it.

Building Blocks 2

It's time to add some new building blocks to the mix. As before, it will be just six new ones. Here they are:

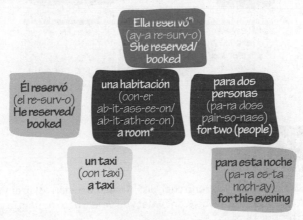

Ella reservó⁵
(ay-a re-surv-o)
She reserved/ booked

Él reservó
(el re-surv-o)
He reserved/ booked

una habitación
(oon-er ab-it-ass-ee-on/ ab-it-ath-ee-on)
a room*

para dos personas
(pa-ra doss pair-so-nass)
for two (people)

un taxi
(oon taxi)
a taxi

para esta noche
(pa-ra es-ta noch-ay)
for this evening

* literally "a habitation"

Once more, these new building blocks have been put into three piles below and what I want you to do is to again make sentences with them, each time using one building block from the first pile, one from the second, and one from the third. Make as many as you can!

---

5 Have you noticed that the word for "reserved" for "he" and "she" is the same as for "you"? Actually "reservó" can mean either "he reserved", "she reserved" or "you reserved". Normally, the context will make it clear who is being talked about. If, however, you feel it's not clear who is being discussed, or you want to add extra emphasis, you can simply include the relevant word for "he" or "she" or "you" in the sentence. So, "he reserved" can be said simply as "reservó" but, if you feel it isn't entirely clear who you're referring to, or if you want to add emphasis to the fact the "he" is the one doing it, you can add the word for "he" in front and say "él reservó". This makes it extra clear who you're talking about. So "he reserved" can be "reservó" or "él reservó", "she reserved" can be "reservó" or "ella reservó", "you reserved" can be "reservó" or "usted reservó". And the same thing applies to everything else – pasó, preparó, visitó – all of these can mean either "he...", "she..." or "you...". Most of the time, you will just use them by themselves because the context will make it clear who you are talking about but, when it doesn't, simply stick in the relevant word and then there'll be no doubt who you're talking about!

Reservé (re-surv-ay) I reserved/booked

una mesa (oon-er may-ser) a table

para usted (pa-ra oo-stedd) for you

Él reservó (el re-surv-o) He reserved/booked

un taxi (oon taxi) a taxi

para dos personas (pa-ra doss pair-so-nass) for two (people)

Checklist 2

You have now reached your second checklist. Remember, don't skip anything! The checklists are essential if you want what you've learnt to remain in your memory for the long term.

So again, cover up the English words on the right-hand side while you read through the list of Spanish words on the left, trying to recall what they mean in English. If you can go through the entire list, giving the correct English meaning for each of the Spanish words / expressions **without making more than three mistakes in total**, then you're done. If not, then go through the list again. Keep doing this, either working from the top of the list to the bottom or from the bottom to the top (it doesn't matter which) until you can do it **without making more than three mistakes**.

Okay. Ready, set, go!

el fin de semana (el fin dey sem-arn-er)	the weekend
romántico (roe-man-tick-oh)	romantic
típico (tip-ick-oh)	typical
político (po-li-tick-oh)	political
lógico (lo-hee-koh)	logical
histórico (ee-sto-rick-oh)	historical
crítico (kri-tick-oh)	critical

clásico (clas-ick-oh)	classical
eléctrico (el-ek-trick-oh)	electrical
idéntico (ee-dent-ick-oh)	identical
biológico (bee-oh-lo-hee-koh)	biological
Visité (visit-ay)	I visited
Barcelona (bar-sair-loan-er / bar-thair-loan-er)	Barcelona
Madrid (ma-drid)	Madrid
Visité Madrid. (visit-ay ma-drid)	I visited Madrid.
Pasé (pass-ay)	I spent
Pasó (pass-o)	You spent
Pasamos (pass-arm-oss)	We spent
septiembre (sep-tee-em-brey)	September
la Navidad (la na-vee-dad)	Christmas (literally "the Christmas")
en Barcelona (en bar-sair-loan-er / bar-thair-loan-er)	in Barcelona
en España (en es-pan-ya)	in Spain
en México (en me-hee-koe)	in Mexico
Pasamos la Navidad en México. (pass-arm-oss la na-vee-dad en me-hee-koe)	We spent Christmas in Mexico.
Pasó septiembre en España. (pass-o sep-tee-em-brey en es-pan-ya)	You spent September in Spain.
y (ee)	and
fue (fway)	it was
fue romántico (fway roe-man-tick-oh)	it was romantic
adorable (ad-or-arb-lay)	lovely / adorable
fue adorable (fway ad-or-arb-lay)	it was lovely / it was adorable
Pasé el fin de semana en Barcelona… y fue adorable. (pass-ay el fin dey sem-arn-er en bar-sair-loan-er / bar-thair-loan-er ee fway ad-or-arb-lay)	I spent the weekend in Barcelona… and it was lovely.

invitación (in-vit-ass-ee-on)	invitation
Invité (in-vit-ay)	I invited
preparación (pray-par-ass-ee-on / pray-par-ath-ee-on)	preparation
Preparé (pre-par-ay)	I prepared
reservación[6] (re-surv-ass-ee-on / re-surv-ath-ee-on)	reservation (preferred in Latin American)
reserva (re-surv-a)	reservation (preferred in Spain)
Reservé (re-surv-ay)	I reserved / booked
cooperación (cope-air-ass-ee-on / cope-air-ath-ee-on)	cooperation
Cooperé[7] (cope-air-ay)	I cooperated
imaginación (im-a-hin-ass-ee-on / im-a-hin-ath-ee-on)	imagination
Imaginé (im-a-hin-ay)	I imagined
manipulación (man-ip-ool-ass-ee-on / man-ip-ool-ath-ee-on)	manipulation
Manipulé (man-ip-ool-ay)	I manipulated
continuación (con-tin-oo-ass-ee-on / con-tin-oo-ath-ee-on)	continuation
Continué (con-tin-oo-ay)	I continued
participación (par-tis-ip-ass-ee-on / par-tith-ip-ath-ee-on)	participation
Participé (par-tis-ip-ay / par-tith-ip-ay)	I participated
exageración (ex-a-hair-ass-ee-on / ex-a-hair-ath-ee-on)	exaggeration
Exageré (ex-a-hair-ay)	I exaggerated

6   You will actually hear "reservación" used much more frequently in Latin American countries. In Spain, you are more likely to hear "reserva" (re-surv-a) used to mean "reservation". Of course, both "reservación" and "reserva" will be understood wherever you go though, so this is nothing major to worry about. However, from now on I will include each of them in your check lists so that you can learn both.

7   The more practice you have turning "ación" / "ation" words into the past tense in Spanish, the better you will get at it. You will receive plenty of practice here but you can also try experimenting with examples of your own. This technique really will let you steal hundreds of Spanish words in minutes. Use it to the full!

admiración (ad-mi-rass-ee-on / ad-mi-rath-ee-on)	admiration
Admiré (ad-mi-ray)	I admired
irritación (ee-ri-tass-ee-on / ee-ri-tath-ee-on)	irritation
Irrité (ee-ri-tay)	I irritated
conversación (con-vair-sass-ee-on / con-vair-sath-ee-on)	conversation
Conversé (con-vair-say)	I conversed
Ordené[8] (or-den-ay)	I ordered (preferred in Latin American)
Pedí (pe-dee)	I ordered (literally "I asked for") – (preferred in Spain) .
Pagué (pag-ay)	I paid
Hice (ee-say / ee-thay)	I did
la cuenta (la kwen-ta)	the bill
la cena (la say-ner / thay-ner)	the dinner
sopa (soap-er)	soup
una mesa (oon-er may-ser)	a table
una habitación (oon-er ab-it-ass-ee-on / ab-it-ath-ee-on)	a room
un taxi (oon taxi)	a taxi
Preparé la cena. (pre-par-ay la say-ner / thay-ner)	I prepared the dinner.
Ordené sopa para la cena. (or-den-ay soap-er pa-ra la say-ner / thay-ner)	I ordered soup for dinner. (preferred in Latin American)
Pedí sopa para la cena (pe-dee soap-er pa-ra la say-ner / thay-ner)	I ordered soup for dinner. (preferred in Spain)
Reservé una mesa para usted. (re-surv-ay oon-er may-ser pa-ra oo-stedd)	I booked a table for you.

8   Just as with "reservación" you will actually hear "ordené" used much more frequently in Latin American countries. In Spain, you are more likely to hear "pedí" (pe-dee), meaning "I asked for", being used as the way to say "I ordered". Both "ordené" and " pedí " will be understood wherever you go though, so again this is nothing major to worry about. I will include each of them in your checklists from now on though so that you can learn both. .

Ella reservó (ay-a re-surv-o)	She booked / reserved
Ella reservó una mesa para esta noche. (ay-a re-surv-ay oon-er may-ser pa-ra es-ta noch-ay)	She booked / reserved a table for this evening.
Él reservó (el re-surv-o)	He booked / reserved
Él reservó una habitación para dos personas. (el re-surv-o oon-er ab-it-ass-ee-on / ab-it-ath-ee-on pa-ra doss pair-so-nass)	He booked / reserved a room for two people.
¿Qué? (kay)	What?
¿Qué preparó? (kay pre-par-o)	What did you prepare?
¿Qué preparó usted? (kay pre-par-o oo-sted)	What did you prepare?
¿Qué hizo usted? (kay ee-soe / ee-thoe oo-sted)	What did you do?
Reservé una mesa, ordené la cena y luego pagué la cuenta. ¿Qué hizo usted? (re-surv-ay oon-er may-ser, or-den-ay la say-ner / thay-ner ee loo-way-go pag-ay la kwen-ta. kay ee-soe / ee-thoe oo-sted)	I booked a table, ordered dinner and then paid the bill. What did you do?

Now, do the same thing again below, except that this time you'll be reading through the list of English words and trying to recall the Spanish. All you need to do is to be able to do one full read-through of them without making more than three mistakes in total and you're done!

the weekend	el fin de semana (el fin dey sem-arn-er)
romantic	romántico (roe-man-tick-oh)
typical	típico (tip-ick-oh)
political	político (po-li-tick-oh)
logical	lógico (lo-hee-koh)
historical	histórico (ee-sto-rick-oh)
critical	crítico (kri-tick-oh)
classical	clásico (clas-ick-oh)

electrical	eléctrico (el-ek-trick-oh)
identical	idéntico (ee-dent-ick-oh)
biological	biológico (bee-oh-lo-hee-koh)
I visited	Visité (visit-ay)
Barcelona	Barcelona (bar-sair-loan-er / bar-thair-loan-er)
Madrid	Madrid (ma-drid)
I visited Madrid.	Visité Madrid. (visit-ay ma-drid)
I spent	Pasé (pass-ay)
You spent	Pasó (pass-o)
We spent	Pasamos (pass-arm-oss)
September	septiembre (sep-tee-em-brey)
Christmas	la Navidad (la na-vee-dad)
in Barcelona	en Barcelona (en bar-sair-loan-er / bar-thair-loan-er)
in Spain	en España (en es-pan-ya)
in Mexico	en México (en me-hee-koe)
We spent Christmas in Mexico.	Pasamos la Navidad en México. (pass-arm-oss la na-vee-dad en me-hee-koe)
You spent September in Spain.	Pasó septiembre en España. (pass-o sep-tee-em-brey en es-pan-ya)
and	y (ee)
it was	fue (fway)
it was romantic	fue romántico (fway roe-man-tick-oh)
lovely / adorable	adorable (ad-or-arb-lay)
it was lovely / it was adorable	fue adorable (fway ad-or-arb-lay)
I spent the weekend in Barcelona… and it was lovely.	Pasé el fin de semana en Barcelona… y fue adorable. (pass-ay el fin dey sem-arn-er en bar-sair-loan-er / bar-thair-loan-er ee fway ad-or-arb-lay)
invitation	invitación (in-vit-ass-ee-on)

I invited	Invité (in-vit-ay)
preparation	preparación (pray-par-ass-ee-on)
I prepared	Preparé (pre-par-ay)
reservation (preferred in Latin American)	reservación (re-surv-ass-ee-on / re-surv-ath-ee-on)
reservation (preferred in Spain)	reserva (re-surv-a)
I reserved / booked	Reservé (re-surv-ay)
cooperation	cooperación (cope-air-ass-ee-on / cope-air-ath-ee-on)
I cooperated	Cooperé (cope-air-ay)
imagination	imaginación (im-a-hin-ass-ee-on / im-a-hin-ath-ee-on)
I imagined	Imaginé (im-a-hin-ay)
manipulation	manipulación (man-ip-ool-ass-ee-on / man-ip-ool-ath-ee-on)
I manipulated	Manipulé (man-ip-ool-ay)
continuation	continuación (con-tin-oo-ass-ee-on / con-tin-oo-ath-ee-on)
I continued	Continué (con-tin-oo-ay)
participation	participación (par-tis-ip-ass-ee-on / par-tith-ip-ath-ee-on)
I participated	Participé (par-tis-ip-ay / par-tith-ip-ay)
exaggeration	exageración (ex-a-hair-ass-ee-on / ex-a-hair-ath-ee-on)
I exaggerated	Exageré (ex-a-hair-ay)
admiration	admiración (ad-mi-rass-ee-on / ad-mi-rath-ee-on)
I admired	Admiré (ad-mi-ray)
irritation	irritación (ee-ri-tass-ee-on / ee-ri-tath-ee-on)
I irritated	Irrité (ee-ri-tay)
conversation	conversación (con-vair-sass-ee-on / con-vair-sath-ee-on)

I conversed	**Conversé** (con-vair-say)
I ordered (preferred in Latin American)	**Ordené** (or-den-ay)
I ordered (literally "I asked for") – (preferred in Spain)	**Pedí** (pe-dee)
I paid	**Pagué** (pag-ay)
I did	**Hice** (ee-say / ee-thay)
the bill	**la cuenta** (la kwen-ta)
the dinner	**la cena** (la say-ner / thay-ner)
soup	**sopa** (soap-er)
a table	**una mesa** (oon-er may-ser)
a room	**una habitación** (oon-er ab-it-ass-ee-on / ab-it-ath-ee-on)
a taxi	**un taxi** (oon taxi)
I prepared the dinner.	**Preparé la cena.** (pre-par-ay la say-ner / thay-ner)
I ordered soup for dinner. (preferred in Latin American)	**Ordené sopa para la cena.** (or-den-ay soap-er pa-ra la say-ner / thay-ner)
I ordered soup for dinner. (preferred in Spain)	**Pedí sopa para la cena.** (pe-dee soap-er pa-ra la say-ner / thay-ner)
I booked a table for you.	**Reservé una mesa para usted.** (re-surv-ay oon-er may-ser pa-ra oo-stedd)
She booked / reserved	**Ella reservó** (ay-a re-surv-o)
She booked / reserved a table for this evening.	**Ella reservó una mesa para esta noche.** (ay-a re-surv-ay oon-er may-ser pa-ra es-ta noch-ay)
He booked / reserved	**Él reservó** (el re-surv-o)
He booked / reserved a room for two people.	**Él reservó una habitación para dos personas.** (el re-surv-o oon-er ab-it-ass-ee-on / ab-it-ath-ee-on pa-ra doss pair-so-nass)
What?	**¿Qué?** (kay)
What did you prepare?	**¿Qué preparó?** (kay pre-par-o)

What did you prepare?	¿Qué preparó usted? (kay pre-par-o oo-sted)
What did you do?	¿Qué hizo usted? (kay ee-soe / ee-thoe oo-sted)
I booked a table, ordered dinner and then paid the bill. What did you do?	Reservé una mesa, ordené la cena y luego pagué la cuenta. ¿Qué hizo usted? (re-surv-ay oon-er may-ser, or-den-ay la say-ner / thay-ner ee loo-way-go pag-ay la kwen-ta. kay ee-soe / ee-thoe oo-sted)

Well, that's it, you're done with Chapter 2! Remember, don't try to hold onto or remember anything you've learnt here. Everything you learn in earlier chapters will be brought back up and reinforced in later chapters. You don't need to do anything or make any effort to memorise anything. The book has been organised in such a way that it will do that for you. So, off you go now and have a rest, please!

Between Chapters Tip!

Stop while you're still enjoying it!

Arnold Schwarzenegger once said that the key to his body-building success was that he stopped his work-out each day just before it started to get boring. On the few occasions he went past that point, he found it incredibly hard to return to the gym again the next day – and he loved working out.

So, as you will almost certainly recall, Tip 1 suggested that you should study every day – which you definitely should do if you can. But that doesn't mean that you should overdo it. So, if you're not really in the mood, just do five minutes. If you are in the mood, though, don't push yourself too hard. Stop before you get to the point where it doesn't feel fun any longer. Best to leave yourself feeling hungry for more rather than bloated and fed up!

CHAPTER 3

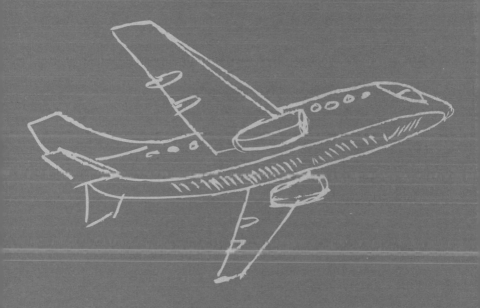

I'm scared of flying, so I'm planning to take the Eurostar.

> **Person 1:**   I'm planning to go back to Spain in May.
>
> **Person 2:**   Really?
>
> **Person 1:**   Yes, I feel like going back to Barcelona but I'm scared of flying, so I'm planning to take the Eurostar.

The brief conversation above does not seem complicated in English and yet, even if you have studied Spanish before, you might well find it impossible to know exactly where to begin in order to express all of this in Spanish. By the end of this chapter, you will have learnt how to carry out both sides of this conversation, plus a great deal more.

Let's begin!

"I have" in Spanish is:

Tengo
(ten-go)

Now, do you remember from the previous Building Blocks section, what "a room" (literally "a habitation") is in Spanish?

una habitación
(oon-er ab-it-ass-ee-on / ab-it-ath-ee-on)

So, how would you say "I have a room"?

Tengo una habitación.
(ten-go oon-er ab-it-ass-ee-on / ab-it-ath-ee-on)

What is "for this evening" in Spanish?

para esta noche
(pa-ra es-ta noch-ay)

So how would you say "I have a room for this evening"?

Tengo una habitación para esta noche.
(ten-go oon-er ab-it-ass-ee-on / ab-it-ath-ee-on pa-ra es-ta noch-ay)

Now again, what is "I reserved" or "I booked"?

Reservé
(re-surv-ay)

And how would you say "I reserved a room" / "I booked a room"?

Reservé una habitación.
(re-surv-ay oon-er ab-it-ass-ee-on / ab-it-ath-ee-on)

"I reserved" or "I booked" is "reservé". "To reserve" or "to book" in Spanish is:

reservar
(re-surv-ar)

So how would you say "to reserve a room" / "to book a room"?

reservar una habitación
(re-surv-ar oon-er ab-it-ass-ee-on / ab-it-ath-ee-on)

Now again, what is "I have" in Spanish?

Tengo
(ten-go)

"The intention" in Spanish is:

la intención
(la in-ten-see-on / in-ten-thee-on)

So, how would you say "I have the intention"?

Tengo la intención
(ten-go la in-ten-see-on / in-ten-thee-on)

The word for "of" in Spanish is:

de
(dey)

So, how would you say "I have the intention of"?

Tengo la intención de
(ten-go la in-ten-see-on / in-ten-thee-on dey)

Now, saying "I have the intention of" is actually one way of saying "I'm planning to..." in Spanish.

With this in mind, how would you say "I'm planning to book a room" (literally "I have the intention of to book a room")?

Tengo la intención de reservar una habitación.
(ten-go la in-ten-see-on / in-ten-thee-on dey re-surv-ar oon-er ab-it-ass-ee-on / ab-it-ath-ee-on)

And how about "I'm planning to book a room for this evening"?

Tengo la intención de reservar una habitación para esta noche.
(ten-go la in-ten-see-on / in-ten-thee-on dey re-surv-ar oon-er ab-it-ass-ee-on / ab-it-ath-ee-on pa-ra es-ta noch-ay)

What is "a table" in Spanish?

una mesa
(oon-er may-ser)

So how would you say "I'm planning to book a table for this evening" (literally "I have the intention of to reserve a table for this evening")?

Tengo la intención de reservar una mesa para esta noche.
(ten-go la in-ten-see-on / in-ten-thee-on dey re-surv-ar oon-er may-ser pa-ra es-ta noch-ay)

"To go back" in Spanish is:

volver
(vol-vair)

Now "volver" (to go back) may at first look like a totally unfamiliar word to you but actually it isn't. You can in fact see it inside the English word "revolver" for example. And also, part of it, inside the word "revolving".

And, if you think about both a revolving door, or the part of a revolver that holds the bullets, both of these turn around and eventually *go back* to where they began.

So, volver, to go back – to revolve back to where you started.

Now that you know that "to go back" is "volver", how would you say "I'm planning to go back"?

Tengo la intención de volver.
(ten-go la in-ten-see-on / in-ten-thee-on dey vol-vair)

"To Spain" is:

a España
(a es-pan-ya)

And so how would you say "I'm planning to go back to Spain"?

Tengo la intención de volver a España.
(ten-go la in-ten-see-on / in-ten-thee-on dey vol-vair a es-pan-ya)

"In May" in Spanish is:

en mayo
(en my-oh)

So, how would you say, "I'm planning to go back to Spain in May"?

Tengo la intención de volver a España en mayo
(ten-go la in-ten-see-on / in-ten-thee-on dey vol-vair a es-pan-ya en my-oh)

So, in Spanish, to say "I'm planning to..." we can simply use "I have the intention of...".

This is an extremely useful expression and actually is just one of a number of extremely useful expressions that work in more or less the same way.

For example, if you want to say "I feel like..." or "I fancy..." in Spanish, you will say "I have desire of..." which in Spanish is:

Tengo ganas de
(ten-go ga-nas dey)

Knowing this now, how would you say "I feel like going back to Spain in May" / "I fancy going back to Spain in May" (literally "I have desire of to go back to Spain in May")?

Tengo ganas de volver a España en mayo.
(ten-go ga-nas dey vol-vair a es-pan-ya en my-oh)

What is "September" in Spanish?

septiembre
(sep-tee-em-brey)

So how would you say "in September"?

en septiembre
(en sep-tee-em-brey)

And how would you say "I feel like going back to Spain in September" / "I fancy going back to Spain in September" (literally "I have desire of to go back to Spain in September")?

Tengo ganas de volver a España en septiembre.
(ten-go ga-nas dey vol-vair a es-pan-ya en sep-tee-em-brey)

And once again, what is "to Spain"?

a España
(a es-pan-ya)

And so how would you say "to Barcelona"?

a Barcelona
(a bar-sair-loan-er / bar-thair-loan-er)

And how would you say "I feel like going back to Barcelona" / "I fancy going back to Barcelona"?

Tengo ganas de volver a Barcelona.
(ten-go ga-nas dey vol-vair a bar-sair-loan-er / bar-thair-loan-er)

You have now learnt two phrases that are constructed in a similar way. The first uses the words "I have the intention of…" to express "I'm planning to…" and the other uses the words "I have desire of…" to mean "I feel like…" or "I fancy…".

Let's add another similar expression to this mix. But again, don't worry about trying to memorise any of this. As you work your way through the rest of the chapter, you'll find that everything comes up again and again, jolting your memory each time and helping those words and phrases stick without resorting to memorisation or learning by rote.

So, as I say, don't worry about making any particular effort to remember, just carry on through the chapter so that you can be reminded of these things when the time is right.

Now, to say "I'm scared of…" in Spanish, you will literally say "I have fear of…", which is:

Tengo miedo de…
(ten-go mee-ed-oh dey)

So, how would you say "I'm scared of going back to Barcelona" (literally "I have fear of to go back to Barcelona")?

Tengo miedo de volver a Barcelona.
(ten-go mee-ed-oh dey vol-vair a bar-sair-loan-er / bar-thair-loan-er)

What about "I'm scared of going back to Spain"?

Tengo miedo de volver a España.
(ten-go mee-ed-oh dey vol-vair a es-pan-ya)

And "I'm scared of going back to Spain in September"?

Tengo miedo de volver a España en septiembre.
(ten-go mee-ed-oh dey vol-vair a es-pan-ya en sep-tee-em-brey)

"To fly" in Spanish is:

volar
(vol-ar)

So, how would you say "I'm scared of flying" (literally "I have fear of to fly")?

Tengo miedo de volar.
(ten-go mee-ed-oh dey vol-ar)

The word for "but" in Spanish is:

pero
(pair-o)

So, how would you say "...but I'm scared of flying"?

...pero tengo miedo de volar
(...pair-o ten-go mee-ed-oh dey vol-ar)

And again, how would you say "I feel like going back to Barcelona" / "I fancy going back to Barcelona" (literally "I have desire of to go back to Barcelona")?

Tengo ganas de volver a Barcelona.
(ten-go ga-nas dey vol-vair a bar-sair-loan-er / bar-thair-loan-er)

Now, let's put those bits together and say "I feel like going back to Barcelona but I'm scared of flying":

Tengo ganas de volver a Barcelona, pero tengo miedo de volar.
(ten-go ga-nas dey vol-vair a bar-sair-loan-er / bar-thair-loan-er pair-o ten-go mee-ed-oh dey vol-ar)

Good. So again, how would you say "I feel like..." / "I fancy..." / "I have desire of..."?

Tengo ganas de...
(ten-go ga-nas dey)

And how would you say "I'm scared of..." / "I have fear of..."?

Tengo miedo de...
(ten-go mee-ed-oh dey)

And can you remember how to say "I'm planning to..." / "I have the intention of..."?

Tengo la intención de...
(ten-go la in-ten-see-on / in-ten-thee-on dey)

"To take" in Spanish is:

tomar
(to-mar)

And "the Eurostar" in Spanish is quite simply:

el Eurostar
(el e-oo-roe-star)

So how would you say "to take the Eurostar"?

tomar el Eurostar
(to-mar el e-oo-roe-star)

And so how would you say "I'm planning to take the Eurostar"?

Tengo la intención de tomar el Eurostar.
(ten-go la in-ten-see-on / in-ten-thee-on dey to-mar el e-oo-roe-star)

"So" in Spanish is:

por lo que
(poor-low-kay)

So, how would you say "…so I'm planning to take the Eurostar"?

…por lo que tengo la intención de tomar el Eurostar.
(poor-low-kay ten-go la in-ten-see-on / in-ten-thee-on dey to-mar el
e-oo-roe-star)

And again, how would you say "I'm frightened of flying"?

Tengo miedo de volar.
(ten-go mee-ed-oh dey vol-ar)

And so how would you say "I'm frightened of flying so I'm planning to take the
Eurostar"?

Tengo miedo de volar, por lo que tengo la intención de tomar el Eurostar.
(ten-go mee-ed-oh dey vol-ar, poor-low-kay ten-go la in-ten-see-on /
in-ten-thee-on dey to-mar el e-oo-roe-star)

And again, how would you say "I feel like…" / "I fancy…" in Spanish?

Tengo ganas de…
(ten-go ga-nas dey)

Extend this now, saying "I feel like going back to Barcelona":

Tengo ganas de volver a Barcelona.
(ten-go ga-nas dey vol-vair a bar-sair-loan-er / bar-thair-loan-er)

And remind me, what is "but" in Spanish?

pero
(pair-o)

Okay, how would you say, "I feel like going back to Barcelona but I'm scared of flying, so I'm planning to take the Eurostar"? Take your time with this sentence, building it slowly, bit by bit, and think out each part as you work through it.

Tengo ganas de volver a Barcelona, pero tengo miedo de volar, por lo que tengo la intención de tomar el Eurostar.
(ten-go ga-nas dey vol-vair a bar-sair-loan-er / bar-thair-loan-er pair-o ten-go mee-ed-oh dey vol-ar, poor-low-kay ten-go la in-ten-see-on / in-ten-thee-on dey to-mar el e-oo-roe-star)

It's a long and complex sentence, so feel free to go through it a few times even once you get it right.

Now let's try putting this together with the rest of the dialogue that we had at the beginning of the chapter. You already know almost everything you need for it.

Start by being Person 1 from the dialogue and say "I feel like going back to Spain in May":

Tengo ganas de volver a España en mayo.
(ten-go ga-nas dey vol-vair a es-pan-ya en my-oh)

Person 2 is now going to reply to this simply by saying "really?". "Really?" in Spanish is literally "of truth?" which is:

¿De verdad?
(dey vair-dad)

So, reply to that earlier statement saying simply "really?" / "of truth?":

¿De verdad?
(dey vair-dad)

"Yes" in Spanish is:

Sí
(see)

So reply to Person 2, saying "Yes, I feel like going back to Barcelona but I'm scared of flying, so I'm planning to take the Eurostar." How will you say that? Again, take your time:

Sí, tengo ganas de volver a Barcelona, pero tengo miedo de volar, por lo que tengo la intención de tomar el Eurostar.
(see ten-go ga-nas dey vol-vair a bar-sair-loan-er / bar-thair-loan-er pair-o ten-go mee-ed-oh dey vol-ar, poor-low-kay ten-go la in-ten-see-on / in-ten-thee-on dey to-mar el e-oo-roe-star)

Good. Now, with that done, try going through the dialogue all in one go below:

I'm planning to go back to Spain in May.
Tengo la intención de volver a España en mayo.
(ten-go la in-ten-see-on / in-ten-thee-on dey vol-vair a es-pan-ya en my-oh)

Really?
¿De verdad?
(dey vair-dad)

Yes, I feel like going back to Barcelona but I'm scared of flying, so I'm planning to take the Eurostar.
Sí, tengo ganas de volver a Barcelona, pero tengo miedo de volar, por lo que tengo la intención de tomar el Eurostar.
(see ten-go ga-nas dey vol-vair a bar-sair-loan-er / bar-thair-loan-er pair-o ten-go mee-ed-oh dey vol-ar, poor-low-kay ten-go la in-ten-see-on / in-ten-thee-on dey to-mar el e-oo-roe-star)

That was an extremely complex dialogue with a lot of different ideas and phrases in it that needed to be juggled. If you felt unclear on how to construct any of the different parts it was made up of, do go back to the beginning of the chapter. And you should feel free to do this at any point when you feel constructing a sentence is becoming a struggle. There is no rush. You should always only work at a pace that feels suitable to you. And, when you do get to the point where you can get through this entire dialogue without making mistakes, it can still be worth practising it a few times. This will help to build your fluency and confidence in using what you've learnt.

If you've done all that, then prepare to get excited as we are now going to expand and develop this dialogue even further as we venture into the next chapter!

It's time again to add some new building blocks. Here they are:

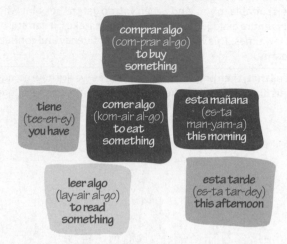

So, you have your new building blocks. Make as many sentences as you can!

* literally "desire of"

You know what to do with the checklist now, so you don't need any reminding about that.

Do bear one thing in mind though. The checklists don't need to be done in one sitting. So, if you get through a page or two and feel that's enough, then simply leave the rest until the next day. Always work at your own pace and don't do so much that you end up feeling overwhelmed. "Steady as she goes" should be your mantra!

el fin de semana (el fin dey sem-arn-er)	the weekend
romántico (roe-man-tick-oh)	romantic
típico (tip-ick-oh)	typical
político (po-li-tick-oh)	political
lógico (lo-hee-koh)	logical
histórico (ee-sto-rick-oh)	historical
crítico (kri-tick-oh)	critical
clásico (clas-ick-oh)	classical
eléctrico (el-ek-trick-oh)	electrical
idéntico (ee-dent-ick-oh)	identical
biológico (bee-oh-lo-hee-koh)	biological
Visité (visit-ay)	I visited
Barcelona (bar-sair-loan-er / bar-thair-loan-er)	Barcelona
Madrid (ma-drid)	Madrid
Visité Madrid. (visit-ay ma-drid)	I visited Madrid.
Pasé (pass-ay)	I spent
Pasó (pass-o)	You spent
Pasamos (pass-arm-oss)	We spent
septiembre (sep-tee-em-brey)	September
la Navidad (la na-vee-dad)	Christmas (literally "the Christmas")
en Barcelona (en bar-sair-loan-er / bar-thair-loan-er)	in Barcelona
en España (en es-pan-ya)	in Spain

en México (en me-hee-koe)	in Mexico
Pasamos la Navidad en México. (pass-arm-oss la na-vee-dad en me-hee-koe)	We spent Christmas in Mexico.
Pasó septiembre en España. (pass-o sep-tee-em-brey en es-pan-ya)	You spent September in Spain.
y (ee)	and
fue (fway)	it was
fue romántico (fway roe-man-tick-oh)	it was romantic
adorable (ad-or-arb-lay)	lovely / adorable
fue adorable (fway ad-or-arb-lay)	it was lovely / it was adorable
Pasé el fin de semana en Barcelona... y fue adorable. (pass-ay el fin dey sem-arn-er en bar-sair-loan-er / bar-thair-loan-er ee fway ad-or-arb-lay)	I spent the weekend in Barcelona... and it was lovely.
invitación (in-vit-ass-ee-on)	invitation
Invité (in-vit-ay)	I invited
preparación (pray-par-ass-ee-on)	preparation
Preparé (pre-par-ay)	I prepared
reservación (re-surv-ass-ee-on / re-surv-ath-ee-on)	reservation (preferred in Latin American)
reserva (re-surv-a)	reservation (preferred in Spain)
Reservé (re-surv-ay)	I reserved / booked
cooperación (cope-air-ass-ee-on / cope-air-ath-ee-on)	cooperation
Cooperé (cope-air-ay)	I cooperated
imaginación (im-a-hin-ass-ee-on / im-a-hin-ath-ee-on)	imagination
Imaginé (im-a-hin-ay)	I imagined
manipulación (man-ip-ool-ass-ee-on / man-ip-ool-ath-ee-on)	manipulation
Manipulé (man-ip-ool-ay)	I manipulated
continuación (con-tin-oo-ass-ee-on / con-tin-oo-ath-ee-on)	continuation

Continué (con-tin-oo-ay)	I continued
participación (par-tis-ip-ass-ee-on / par-tith-ip-ath-ee-on)	participation
Participé (par-tis-ip-ay / par-tith-ip-ay)	I participated
exageración (ex-a-hair-ass-ee-on / ox a hair ath ee on)	exaggeration
Exageré (ex-a-hair-ay)	I exaggerated
admiración (ad-mi-rass-ee-on / ad-mi-rath-ee-on)	admiration
Admiré (ad-mi-ray)	I admired
irritación (ee-ri-tass-ee-on / ee-ri-tath-ee-on)	irritation
Irrité (ee-ri-tay)	I irritated
conversación (con-vair-sass-ee-on / con-vair-sath-ee-on)	conversation
Conversé (con-vair-say)	I conversed
ordené (or-den-ay)	I ordered (preferred in Latin American)
Pedí (pe-dee)	I ordered (literally "I asked for") – (preferred in Spain)
pagué (pag-ay)	I paid
Hice (ee-say / ee-thay)	I did
la cuenta (la kwen-ta)	the bill
la cena (la say-ner / thay-ner)	the dinner
sopa (soap-er)	soup
una mesa (oon-er may-ser)	a table
una habitación (oon-er ab-it-ass-ee-on / ab-it-ath-ee-on)	a room
un taxi (oon taxi)	a taxi
Preparé la cena. (pre-par-ay la say-ner / thay-ner)	I prepared the dinner.
Ordené sopa para la cena. (or-den-ay soap-er pa-ra la say-ner / thay-ner)	I ordered soup for dinner. (preferred in Latin American)
Pedí sopa para la cena. (pe-dee soap-er pa-ra la say-ner / thay-ner)	I ordered soup for dinner (preferred in Spain)

Reservé una mesa para usted. (re-surv-ay oon-er may-ser pa-ra oo-stedd)	I booked a table for you.
Ella reservó (ay-a re-surv-o)	She booked / reserved
Ella reservó una mesa para esta noche. (ay-a re-surv-ay oon-er may-ser pa-ra es-ta noch-ay)	She booked / reserved a table for this evening.
Él reservó (el re-surv-o)	He booked / reserved
Él reservó una habitación para dos personas. (el re-surv-o oon-er ab-it-ass-ee-on / ab-it-ath-ee-on pa-ra doss pair-so-nass)	He booked / reserved a room for two people.
¿Qué? (kay)	What?
¿Qué preparó? (kay pre-par-o)	What did you prepare?
¿Qué preparó usted? (kay pre-par-o oo-sted)	What did you prepare?
¿Qué hizo usted? (kay ee-soe / ee-thoe oo-sted)	What did you do?
Reservé una mesa, ordené la cena y luego pagué la cuenta. ¿Qué hizo usted? (re-surv-ay oon-er may-ser, or-den-ay la say-ner / thay-ner ee loo-way-go pag-ay la kwen-ta. kay ee-soe / ee-thoe oo-sted)	I booked a table, ordered dinner and then paid the bill. What did you do?
Tengo la intención de… (ten-go la in-ten-see-on / in-ten-thee-on dey)	I'm planning to… (literally "I have the intention of…")
Tengo la intención de volver a España en mayo. (ten-go la in-ten-see-on / in-ten-thee-on dey vol-vair a es-pan-ya en my-oh)	I'm planning to go back to Spain in May.
Tengo miedo de… (ten-go mee-ed-oh dey)	I'm scared of… (literally "I have fear of…")
Tengo miedo de volver a España en septiembre. (ten-go mee-ed-oh dey vol-vair a es-pan-ya en sep-tee-em-brey)	I'm scared of going back to Spain in September.
¿De verdad? (dey vair-dad)	Really?
por lo que (poor-low-kay)	so
pero (pair-o)	but

Tengo ganas de... (ten-go ga-nas dey)	I feel like... / I fancy... (literally "I have desire of...")
Sí, tengo ganas de volver a Barcelona, pero tengo miedo de volar, por lo que tengo la intención de tomar el Eurostar. (see ten-go ga-nas dey vol-vair a bar-sair-loan-er / bar-thair-loan-er pair-o ten-go mee-ed-oh dey vol-ar, poor-low-kay ten-go la in-ten-see-on / in-ten-thee-on dey to-mar el e-oo-roe-star)	Yes, I feel like going back to Barcelona but I'm scared of flying, so I'm planning to take the Eurostar.
Tengo ganas de comprar algo esta mañana. (ten-go ga-nas dey com-prar al-go es-ta man-yarn-a)	I feel like / fancy buying something this morning.
Tengo ganas de leer algo esta tarde. (ten-go ga-nas dey lay-air al-go es-ta tar-dey)	I feel like / fancy reading something this afternoon.
Tiene (tee-en-ey)	You have
Tiene ganas de comer algo esta noche. (tee-en-ey ga-nas dey kom-air al-go)	You feel like eating something this evening.

Now, time to do it the other way around!

the weekend	el fin de semana (el fin dey sem-arn-er)
romantic	romántico (roe-man-tick-oh)
typical	típico (tip-ick-oh)
political	político (po-li-tick-oh)
logical	lógico (lo-hee-koh)
historical	histórico (ee-sto-rick-oh)
critical	crítico (kri-tick-oh)
classical	clásico (clas-ick-oh)
electrical	eléctrico (el-ek-trick-oh)
identical	idéntico (ee-dent-ick-oh)
biological	biológico (bee-oh-lo-hee-koh)
I visited	Visité (visit-ay)

Barcelona	**Barcelona** (bar-sair-loan-er / bar-thair-loan-er)
Madrid	**Madrid** (ma-drid)
I visited Madrid.	**Visité Madrid.** (visit-ay ma-drid)
I spent	**Pasé** (pass-ay)
You spent	**Pasó** (pass-o)
We spent	**Pasamos** (pass-arm-oss)
September	**septiembre** (sep-tee-em-brey)
Christmas (literally "the Christmas")	**la Navidad** (la na-vee-dad)
in Barcelona	**en Barcelona** (en bar-sair-loan-er / bar-thair-loan-er)
in Spain	**en España** (en es-pan-ya)
in Mexico	**en México** (en me-hee-koe)
We spent Christmas in Mexico.	**Pasamos la Navidad en México.** (pass-arm-oss la na-vee-dad en me-hee-koe)
You spent September in Spain.	**Pasó septiembre en España.** (pass-o sep-tee-em-brey en es-pan-ya)
and	**y** (ee)
it was	**fue** (fway)
it was romantic	**fue romántico** (fway roe-man-tick-oh)
lovely / adorable	**adorable** (ad-or-arb-lay)
it was lovely / it was adorable	**fue adorable** (fway ad-or-arb-lay)
I spent the weekend in Barcelona… and it was lovely.	**Pasé el fin de semana en Barcelona… y fue adorable.** (pass-ay el fin dey sem-arn-er en bar-sair-loan-er / bar-thair-loan-er ee fway ad-or-arb-lay)
invitation	**invitación** (in-vit-ass-ee-on)
I invited	**invité** (in-vit-ay)
preparation	**preparación** (pray-par-ass-ee-on)
I prepared	**preparé** (pre-par-ay)
reservation (preferred in Latin American)	**reservación** (re-surv-ass-ee-on / re-surv-ath-ee-on)

reservation (preferred in Spain)	reserva (re-surv-a)
I reserved / booked	Reservé (re-surv-ay)
cooperation	cooperación (cope-air-ass-ee-on / cope-air-ath-ee-on)
I cooperated	Cooperé (cope-air-ay)
imagination	imaginación (im-a-hin-ass-ee-on / im-a-hin-ath-ee-on)
I imagined	Imaginé (im-a-hin-ay)
manipulation	manipulación (man-ip-ool-ass-ee-on / man-ip-ool-ath-ee-on)
I manipulated	Manipulé (man-ip-ool-ay)
continuation	continuación (con-tin-oo-ass-ee-on / con-tin-oo-ath-ee-on)
I continued	Continué (con-tin-oo-ay)
participation	participación (par-tis-ip-ass-ee-on / par-tith-ip-ath-ee-on)
I participated	Participé (par-tis-ip-ay / par-tith-ip-ay)
exaggeration	exageración (ex-a-hair-ass-ee-on / ex-a-hair-ath-ee-on)
I exaggerated	Exageré (ex-a-hair-ay)
admiration	admiración (ad-mi-rass-ee-on / ad-mi-rath-ee-on)
I admired	Admiré (ad-mi-ray)
irritation	irritación (ee-ri-tass-ee-on / ee-ri-tath-ee-on)
I irritated	Irrité (ee-ri-tay)
conversation	conversación (con-vair-sass-ee-on / con-vair-sath-ee-on)
I conversed	Conversé (con-vair-say)
I ordered (preferred in Latin American)	Ordené (or-den-ay)
I ordered (literally "I asked for") – (preferred in Spain)	Pedí (pe-dee)
I paid	Pagué (pag-ay)
I did	Hice (ee-say / ee-thay)

the bill	**la cuenta** (la kwen-ta)
the dinner	**la cena** (la say-ner / thay-ner)
soup	**sopa** (soap-er)
a table	**una mesa** (oon-er may-ser)
a room	**una habitación** (oon-er ab-it-ass-ee-on / ab-it-ath-ee-on)
a taxi	**un taxi** (oon taxi)
I prepared the dinner.	**Preparé la cena.** (pre-par-ay la say-ner / thay-ner)
I ordered soup for dinner. (preferred in Latin American)	**Ordené sopa para la cena.** (or-den-ay soap-er pa-ra la say-ner / thay-ner)
I ordered soup for dinner. (preferred in Spain)	**Pedí sopa para la cena.** (pe-dee soap-er pa-ra la say-ner / thay-ner)
I booked a table for you.	**Reservé una mesa para usted.** (re-surv-ay oon-er may-ser pa-ra oo-stedd)
She booked / reserved	**Ella reservó** (ay-a re-surv-o)
She booked / reserved a table for this evening.	**Ella reservó una mesa para esta noche.** (ay-a re-surv-ay oon-er may-ser pa-ra es-ta noch-ay)
He booked / reserved	**Él reservó** (el re-surv-o)
He booked / reserved a room for two people.	**Él reservó una habitación para dos personas.** (el re-surv-o oon-er ab-it-ass-ee-on / ab-it-ath-ee-on pa-ra doss pair-so-nass)
What?	**¿Qué?** (kay)
What did you prepare?	**¿Qué preparó?** (kay pre-par-o)
What did you prepare?	**¿Qué preparó usted?** (kay pre-par-o oo-sted)
What did you do?	**¿Qué hizo usted?** (kay ee-soe / ee-thoe oo-sted)
I booked a table, ordered dinner and then paid the bill. What did you do?	**Reservé una mesa, ordené la cena y luego pagué la cuenta. ¿Qué hizo usted?** (re-surv-ay oon-er may-ser, or-den-ay la say-ner / thay-ner ee loo-way-go pag-ay la kwen-ta. kay ee-soe / ee-thoe oo-sted)

I'm planning to... (literally "I have the intention of...")	Tengo la intención de... (ten-go la in-ten-see-on / in-ten-thee-on dey)
I'm planning to go back to Spain in May.	Tengo la intención de volver a España en mayo. (ten-go la in-ten-see-on / in-ten-thee-on dey vol-vair a es-pan-ya en my-oh)
I'm scared of... (literally "I have fear of...")	Tengo miedo de... (ten-go mee-ed-oh doy)
I'm scared of going back to Spain in September.	Tengo miedo de volver a España en septiembre. (ten-go mee-ed-oh dey vol-vair a es-pan-ya en sep-tee-em-brey)
Really?	¿De verdad? (dey vair-dad)
so	por lo que (poor-low-kay)
but	pero (pair-o)
I feel like... / I fancy... (literally "I have desire of...")	Tengo ganas de... (ten-go ga-nas dey)
Yes, I feel like going back to Barcelona but I'm scared of flying, so I'm planning to take the Eurostar.	Sí, tengo ganas de volver a Barcelona, pero tengo miedo de volar, por lo que tengo la intención de tomar el Eurostar. (see ten-go ga-nas dey vol-vair a bar-salr-loan-er / bar-thair-loan-er pair-o ten-go mee-ed-oh dey vol-ar. poor-low-kay ten-go la in-ten-see-on / in-ten-thee-on dey to-mar el e-oo-roe-star)
I feel like / fancy buying something this morning.	Tengo ganas de comprar algo esta mañana. (ten-go ga-nas dey com-prar al-go es-ta man-yarn-a)
I feel like / fancy reading something this afternoon.	Tengo ganas de leer algo esta tarde. (ten-go ga-nas dey lay-air al-go es-ta tar-dey)
You have	Tiene (tee-en-ey)
You feel like eating something this evening.	Tiene ganas de comer algo esta noche. (tee-en-ey ga-nas dey kom-air al-go)

Well, that's it, you're done with Chapter 3. Take a break!

How to learn the Spanish days of the week in an easy and meaningful way!

Do you know the days of the week in Spanish? Are you sure?

Well, either way, most people aren't aware what the days of the week actually mean in Spanish. If they were, they might be surprised how much easier to remember, more meaningful and more beautiful they become.

Let's take a look at them!

Monday – lunes

Monday, in English, actually means "Moon's Day" and the same is true in Spanish. The Spanish use their word for moon, which is "luna" (think "lunar") and combine this with the last two letters of the Latin word for "day", giving them with "lunes" – Moonday / Monday.

Tuesday – martes

If Monday in Spanish is dedicated to the moon, Tuesday is dedicated to Mars. So, to make Tuesday in Spanish we take the Spanish word for Mars "Marte", and again combine this with the end of the Latin word for "day", giving us "martes" – Mars's Day / Tuesday.

Wednesday – miércoles

Ah, here we are now at "Wednesday" or "Wodan's Day" as it really should read in English. However, whereas in English Wednesday celebrates the god Wodan, in Spanish it celebrates Mercury, making Wednesday "Mercury's Day" in Spanish – miércoles.

Thursday – jueves

In English, the day after Wodan's Day is of course "Thor's Day", now written "Thursday". In Spain, by contrast, the day belongs to Jove, King of the Gods. Jove's Day in Spanish is "jueves".

Friday – viernes

Friday in English means "Frigga's Day". "Who is Frigga?" you may ask. Well, she was Odin's wife and Thor's mother. She was also, for the earliest English people, the goddess of love. Curiously, Spanish also names Friday after a goddess of love, Venus. So, Friday in Spanish becomes Venus's Day – viernes.

Saturday – sábado

Saturday in English is "Saturn's Day". The Spanish for Saturday, however, simply means "Sabbath", as the Sabbath was originally observed on Saturday rather than Sunday. Saturday in Spanish is therefore "sábado".

Sunday – domingo

I'm sure you can guess the meaning of Sunday in English; clearly it is the Sun's Day. In Spanish, though, its sound comes from Latin again – from "diēs Dominica" – meaning "the day of the Lord". In modern Spanish this has simply become "domingo".

So, there you have the days of the week in Spanish. Hopefully they hold a little more meaning for you than they did before. If you don't know them already, you'll find them on a quick reference list on the next page. Just take a look at it each time you finish a chapter, covering up the Spanish and seeing if you can recall it, and you'll soon pick them up.

(By the way, have you noticed that, unlike in English, days of the week in Spanish don't need to be written with a capital letter?)

Monday	Moon Day	lunes	
Tuesday	Mars Day	martes	
Wednesday	Mercury Day	miércoles	
Thursday	Jove Day	jueves	
Friday	Venus Day	viernes	
Saturday	Sabbath Day	sábado	
Sunday	Day of the Lord	domingo	

CHAPTER 4

You need help, mate!

You need help, mate!

Person 1:	I'm planning to go back to Spain in May.
Person 2:	Really?
Person 1:	Yes, I feel like going back to Barcelona but I'm scared of flying, so I'm planning to take the Eurostar.
Person 2:	Really? You're scared of flying?
Person 1:	Yes, I can't stand flying!
Person 2:	You need help, mate!

As you can see, I have extended the dialogue from the previous chapter. You are now going to learn how to complete this conversation, building on what you've learnt already. You will also expand your range of everyday Spanish expressions as you go.

So, remind me now, how would you say "I'm planning to..."?

Tengo la intención de...
(ten-go la in-ten-see-on / in-ten-thee-on dey)

And how would you say "I'm planning to go back to Spain in May"?

Tengo la intención de volver a España en mayo.
(ten-go la in-ten-see-on / in-ten-thee-on dey vol-vair a es-pan-ya en my-oh)

How would someone reply to that, saying "really"?

¿De verdad?
(dey vair-dad)

And again, what was "I feel like..." in Spanish?

Tengo ganas de...
(ten-go ga-nas dey)

And so how would you say "I feel like going back to Spain" / "I fancy going back to Spain"?

Tengo ganas de volver a España.
(ten-go ga-nas dey vol-vair a es-pan-ya)

How about "I feel like going back to Barcelona" / "I fancy going back to Barcelona"?

Tengo ganas de volver a Barcelona.
(ten-go ga-nas dey vol-vair a bar-sair-loan-er / bar-thair-loan-er)

And how would you say "I'm scared of..." in Spanish?

Tengo miedo de...
(ten-go mee-ed-oh dey)

What about "I'm scared of flying"?

Tengo miedo de volar.
(ten-go mee-ed-oh dey vol-ar)

Finally, just as we ended the previous chapter, give an answer to this saying "Yes, I feel like going back to Barcelona but I'm scared of flying, so I'm planning to take the Eurostar."

Sí, tengo ganas de volver a Barcelona, pero tengo miedo de volar, por lo que tengo la intención de tomar el Eurostar.
(see ten-go ga-nas dey vol-vair a bar-sair-loan-er / bar-thair-loan-er pair-o ten-go mee-ed-oh dey vol-ar, poor-low-kay ten-go la in-ten-see-on / in-ten-thee-on dey to-mar el e-oo-roe-star)

Now, let's expand on this.
"I hate" in Spanish is:

Odio
(*oh-dee-oh*)

Now "odio" may at first look like a totally unfamiliar word to you but actually it isn't. This is because we can find "odio" inside the English word "odious", which means "hateful".

So, how would you say "I hate flying!" (literally "I hate to fly")?

¡Odio volar![9]
(*oh-dee-oh volar*)

What was the word for "Christmas" in Spanish?

la Navidad
(la *na-vee-dad*)

So, how would you say "I hate Christmas!"?

¡Odio la Navidad!
(*oh-dee-oh la na-vee-dad*)

"You hate" is:

Odia
(*oh-dee-a*)

So, how would you say "you hate Christmas!"?

¡Odia la Navidad!
(*oh-dee-a la na-vee-dad*)

How about "you hate flying!"?

¡Odia volar!
(*oh-dee-a vol-ar*)

---

9   Notice how, just like with question marks, Spanish likes to use two exclamation marks. One is placed upside down at the front while the other one goes at the end, normal way up, just like in English.

You can very easily turn this statement "you hate flying!" into a question in Spanish. All you need to do is to raise your voice at the end of the sentence. Doing this, you will ask "you hate flying?" Do that now:

¿Odia volar?
(*oh-dee-a vol-ar*)

Now try "you hate Christmas?":

¿Odia la Navidad?
(*oh-dee-a la na-vee-dad*)

So far we have been using "odia" to say "you hate" in Spanish but this is not the only way to say this.

This is because, in Spanish, there is always a way to say something to someone you are on formal terms with and another way to say it to someone with whom you are on more relaxed, informal terms.

Fortunately, changing from one to the other is simple. All you do is add an "s".

So again, what was "you hate" in Spanish?

Odia
(*oh-dee-a*)

Now, add an "s" onto the end of this to address someone informally and, again, say "you hate" (informal):

Odias
(*oh-dee-ass*)

Do you remember what "you have" was (from the previous Building Blocks section)?

Tiene
(*tee-en-ey*)

This is the formal way to say "you have".

How would you make it informal? What would be "you have" (informal)?

Tienes
(*tee-en-es*)

And how would you say "you feel like going back to Spain" (informal) – (literally "you have desire of to go back to Spain")?

Tienes ganas de volver a España.
(tee-en-es ga-nas dey vol-vair a es-pan-ya)

How would you say "you are scared of…" (informal) – (literally "you have fear of")?

Tienes miedo de…
(tee-en-es mee-ed-oh dey)

How about "you are scared of flying" (informal)?

Tienes miedo de volar.
(tee-en-es mee-ed-oh dey vol-ar)

Turn this into a question now and ask "you are scared of flying?" (informal):

¿Tienes miedo de volar?
(tee-en-es mee-ed-oh dey vol-ar)

Now again, what is "you have" (formal)?

Tiene
(tee-en-ey)

And what is "you have" (informal)?

Tienes
(tee-en-es)

What is "I hate"?

Odio
(ten-go mee-ed-oh dey)

And what is "you hate" (formal)?

Odia
(oh-dee-a)

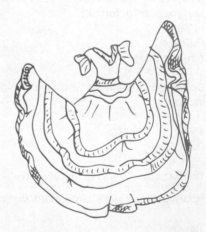

What about "you hate" (informal)?

Odias
(oh-dee-ass)

And so how would you say "you hate Christmas" (informal)?

Odias la Navidad.
(oh-dee-ass la na-vee-dad)

And how would you say "you hate flying" (informal)?

Odias volar.
(oh-dee-ass vol-ar)

And again, how would you say "you're scared of flying" (informal) – (literally "you have fear of flying")?

Tienes miedo de volar.
(tee-en-es mee-ed-oh dey vol-ar)

Turn this into a question by raising your voice at the end of the sentence.
Ask "you're scared of flying?" (informal):

¿Tienes miedo de volar?
(tee-en-es mee-ed-oh dey vol-ar)

Now answer this question, saying "yes, I'm scared of flying!"

Sí, ¡tengo miedo de volar!
(see ten-go mee-ed-oh dey volar)

Good.

So, once more, what is "you hate" (formal)?

Odia
(oh-dee-a)

And "you hate" (informal)?

Odias
(oh-dee-ass)

And what is "I hate"?

Odio
(oh-dee-oh)

"I need" in Spanish is:

Necesito
(ness-e-seet-oh / neth-e-seet-oh)

It's clear to see that the Spanish word for "I need" is related to the English word "necessary" and even more so to the English word "necessity".

So, knowing that "I need" is "necesito" (pronounced "ness-e-seet-oh / neth-e-seet-oh"), how would you say "I need a taxi"?

Necesito un taxi.
(ness-e-seet-oh / neth-e-seet-oh oon taxi)

Now again, what is "a room" in Spanish?

una habitación
(oon-er ab-it-ass-ee-on / ab-it-ath-ee-on)

So how would you say "I need a room"?

Necesito una habitación.
(ness-e-seet-oh / neth-e-seet-oh oon-er ab-it-ass-ee-on / ab-it-ath-ee-on)

"To speak" or "to talk" in Spanish is:

hablar
(a-blar)

So, how would you say "I need to speak"?

Necesito hablar.
(ness-e-seet-oh / neth-e-seet-oh a-blar)

"Spanish" in Spanish is:

español
(es-pa-nyol)

So, how would you say "I need to speak Spanish"?

Necesito hablar español.
(ness-e-seet-oh / neth-e-seet-oh a-blar es-pa-nyol)

"You need" (formal) in Spanish is:

Necesita
(ness-e-seet-a / neth-e-seet-a)

So how would you say "you need to speak Spanish" (formal)?

Necesita hablar español.
(ness-e-seet-a / neth-e-seet-a a-blar es-pa-nyol)

If "you need" (formal) is "necesita", how would you say "you need" (informal)?

Necesitas
(ness-e-seet-ass / neth-e-seet-ass)

Knowing this, how would you say "you need to speak Spanish" (informal)?

Necesitas hablar español.
(ness-e-seet-ass / neth-e-seet-ass a-blar es-pa-nyol)

How about "you need a room" (informal)?

Necesitas una habitación.
(ness-e-seet-ass / neth-e-seet-ass oon-er ab-it-ass-ee-on /
ab-it-ath-ee-on)

What about "you need a taxi" (informal)?

Necesitas un taxi.
(ness-e-seet-ass / neth-e-seet-ass oon taxi)

"Help" in Spanish is literally "aid", which in Spanish is:

ayuda
(a-yoo-der)

So, how would you say "you need help" (informal)?

Necesitas ayuda.
(ness-e-seet-ass / neth-e-seet-ass a-yoo-der)

The word for "mate", "pal", "buddy", and so on, in Spanish is:

camarada
(ca-ma-ra-da)

So, how would you say "you need help, mate!"

¡Necesitas ayuda, camarada!
(ness-e-seet-ass / neth-e-seet-ass a-yoo-der, ca-ma-ra-da)

Alright, let's review some of these phrases again.
First of all, how would you say "I'm planning to..." (literally "I have the intention of")?

Tengo la intención de...
(ten-go la in-ten-see-on / in-ten-thee-on dey)

And how would you say "I feel like..." / "I fancy..." (literally "I have desire of")?

Tengo ganas de...
(ten-go ga-nas dey)

How about "I'm scared of..." (literally "I have fear of")?

Tengo miedo de...
(ten-go mee-ed-oh dey)

And what is "I hate"?

Odio
(oh-dee-oh)

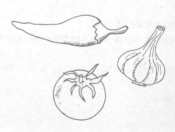

And finally what is "I need"?

Necesito
(ness-e-seet-oh / neth-e-seet-oh)

So, how would you say "I need to speak Spanish"?

Necesito hablar español.
(ness-e-seet-oh / neth-e-seet-oh a-blar es-pa-nyol)

How about "I hate speaking Spanish"?

Odio hablar español.
(oh-dee-oh a-blar es-pa-nyol)

And how would you say "I feel like speaking Spanish"?

Tengo ganas de hablar español.
(ten-go ga-nas dey a-blar es-pa-nyol)

And "I'm scared of speaking Spanish"?

Tengo miedo de hablar español.
(ten-go mee-ed-oh dey a-blar es-pa-nyol)

How about "I'm planning to speak Spanish"?

Tengo la intención de hablar español.
(ten-go la in-ten-see-on / in-ten-thee-on dey a-blar es-pa-nyol)

And how would you say "I'm planning to go back to Spain in May"?

Tengo la intención de volver a España en mayo.
(ten-go la in-ten-see-on / in-ten-thee-on dey vol-vair a es-pan-ya en my-oh)

What about "I'm scared of going back to Spain in May"?

Tengo miedo de volver a España en mayo.
(ten-go mee-ed-oh dey vol-vair a es-pan-ya en my-oh)

And "I feel like going back to Spain in May"?

Tengo ganas de volver a España en mayo.
(ten-go ga-nas dey vol-vair a es-pan-ya en my-oh)

"I need to go back to Spain in May"?

Necesito volver a España en mayo.
(ness-e-seet-oh / neth-e-seet-oh vol-vair a es-pan-ya en my-oh)

Now again, how would you say "I hate flying!"?

¡Odio volar!
(oh-dee-oh volar)

And how would you say "I hate Christmas!"?

¡Odio la Navidad!
(oh-dee-oh la na-vee-dad)

What is "to take"?

tomar
(to-mar)

And how about "to take the Eurostar"?

tomar el Eurostar
(to-mar el e-oo-roe-star)

So how would you say "I hate to take / taking the Eurostar"?

Odio tomar el Eurostar.
(oh-dee-oh to-mar el e-oo-roe-star)

How would someone you said that to ask you "really?"

¿De verdad?
(dey vair-dad)

And how would you say "I'm planning to take the Eurostar"?

Tengo la intención de tomar el Eurostar.
(ten-go la in-ten-see-on / in-ten-thee-on dey to-mar el e-oo-roe-star)

How about "I feel like going back to Barcelona"?

Tengo ganas de volver a Barcelona.
(ten-go ga-nas dey vol-vair a bar-sair-loan-er / bar-thair-loan-er)

And what about "I'm scared of flying"?

Tengo miedo de volar.
(ten-go mee-ed-oh dey vol-ar)

What is the word for "but" in Spanish?

pero
(pair-o)

And how do you say "so"?

por lo que
(poor-low-kay)

So how would you say "I feel like going back to Barcelona but I'm scared of flying, so I'm planning to take the Eurostar"?

Tengo ganas de volver a Barcelona, pero tengo miedo de volar, por lo que tengo la intención de tomar el Eurostar.
(ten-go ga-nas dey vol-vair a bar-sair-loan-er / bar-thair-loan-er pair-o ten-go mee-ed-oh dey vol-ar poor-low-kay ten-go la in-ten-see-on / in-ten-thee-on dey to-mar el e-oo-roe-star)

What is "you have" (informal)?

Tienes
(tee-en-es)

So how would you say informally "you feel like going back to Barcelona" (literally "you have desire of to return to Barcelona")?

Tienes ganas de volver a Barcelona.
(tee-en-es ga-nas dey vol-vair a bar-sair-loan-er / bar-thair-loan-er)

How about "you are scared of flying" (informal)?

Tienes miedo de volar.
(tee-en-es mee-ed-oh dey vol-ar)

Turn this into a question by raising your voice at the end and ask "you are scared of flying?" (informal):

¿Tienes miedo de volar?
(tee-en-es mee-ed-oh dey vol-ar)

How would someone answer "Yes, I hate flying"?

Sí, odio volar.
(see oh-dee-oh volar)

And again, how would you say "I need..."?

Necesito...
(ness-e-seet-oh / neth-e-seet-oh)

How would you say "I need help"?

Necesito ayuda.
(ness-e-seet-oh / neth-e-seet-oh a-yoo-der)

And how would you say informally "You need help"?

Necesitas ayuda.
(ness-e-seet-ass / neth-e-seet-ass a-yoo-der)

Finally, how would you say "mate"?

camarada
(ca-ma-ra-da)

Put this together now and say "you need help, mate!" (informal):

¡Necesitas ayuda, camarada!
(ness-e-seet-ass / neth-e-seet-ass a-yoo-der, ca-ma-ra-da)

Okay, you're ready now to make an attempt at doing the entire dialogue by yourself. Take each sentence slowly and, if you get it wrong, just take another stab at it. It isn't a race and you should just take your time to work it out.

Have a go now:

Person 1:   I'm planning to go back to Spain in May.
              Tengo la intención de volver a España en mayo.
              (ten-go la in-ten-see-on / in-ten-thee-on dey vol-vair a
              es-pan-ya en my-oh)

Person 2:   Really?
              ¿De verdad?
              (dey vair-dad)

Person 1:   Yes, I feel like going back to Barcelona but I'm scared of flying,
              so I'm planning to take the Eurostar.
              Sí, tengo ganas de volver a Barcelona, pero tengo miedo de
              volar, por lo que tengo la intención de tomar el Eurostar.
              (see ten-go ga-nas dey vol-vair a bar-sair-loan-er /
              bar-thair-loan-er pair-o ten-go mee-ed-oh dey vol-ar,
              poor-low-kay ten-go la in-ten-see-on / in-ten-thee-on dey
              to-mar el e-oo-roe-star)

Person 2:   Really? You're scared of flying?
              ¿De verdad? ¿Tienes miedo de volar?
              (dey vair-dad tee-en-es mee-ed-oh dey vol-ar)

Person 1:   Yes, I can't stand flying!
              Sí, ¡odio volar!
              (see oh-dee-oh volar)

Person 2:   You need help, mate!
              ¡Necesitas ayuda, camarada!
              (ness-e-seet-ass / neth-e-seet-ass a-yoo-der,
              ca-ma-ra-da)

How did that go? It's fairly complex stuff but, as you're probably beginning to notice, it is also just a matter of patterns. Learn the patterns and you'll find you can very quickly begin to communicate in the language – with minimum effort!

Now, after all that hard work, why not relax with a little Word Robbery?

·Time to steal some words!
word Robbery Number 3

The third group of words we are going to steal are words that end in "**ary**" in English. These end in "**ario**" in Spanish.

So, "ordin**ary**" becomes "ordin**ario**", "solit**ary**" becomes "solit**ario**", "contr**ary**" becomes "contr**ario**" and so on.

There are actually more than 400 of these in English and we can begin using these in Spanish right away.

Adding them to the words we've already stolen so far, we have now reached a total of 2400 words stolen – and we're only at the end of Chapter 4!

Words stolen so far 2400

Building Blocks 4

Okay. Building block time. Here they are:

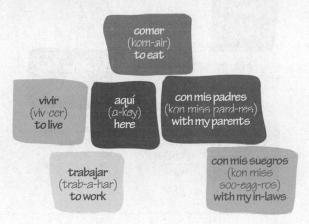

comer
(kom-air)
to eat

vivir
(viv-eer)
to live

aquí
(a-key)
here

con mis padres
(kon miss pard-res)
with my parents

trabajar
(trab-a-har)
to work

con mis suegros
(kon miss
soo-egg-ros)
with my in-laws

As before, let's use the building blocks below to make as many sentences as we can. Make sure to use every word at least once or, preferably, several times!

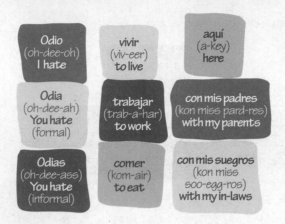

Odio
(oh-dee-oh)
I hate

vivir
(viv-eer)
to live

aquí
(a-key)
here

Odia
(oh-dee-ah)
You hate
(formal)

trabajar
(trab-a-har)
to work

con mis padres
(kon miss pard-res)
with my parents

Odias
(oh-dee-ass)
You hate
(informal)

comer
(kom-air)
to eat

con mis suegros
(kon miss
soo-egg-ros)
with my in-laws

Checklist 4

well, off you go then!

el fin de semana (el fin dey sem-arn-er)	the weekend
romántico (roe-man-tick-oh)	romantic
típico (tip-ick-oh)	typical
político (po-li-tick-oh)	political
lógico (lo-hee-koh)	logical
histórico (ee-sto-rick-oh)	historical
crítico (kri-tick-oh)	critical
clásico (clas-ick-oh)	classical
eléctrico (el-ek-trick-oh)	electrical
idéntico (ee-dent-ick-oh)	identical
biológico (bee-oh-lo-hee-koh)	biological

Visité (visit-ay)	I visited
Barcelona (bar-sair-loan-er / bar-thair-loan-er)	Barcelona
Madrid (ma-drid)	Madrid
Visité Madrid. (visit-ay ma-drid)	I visited Madrid.
Pasé (pass-ay)	I spent
Pasó (pass-o)	You spent
Pasamos (pass-arm-oss)	We spent
septiembre (sep-tee-om-brey)	September
la Navidad (la na-vee-dad)	Christmas (literally "the Christmas")
en Barcelona (en bar-sair-loan-er / bar-thair-loan-er)	in Barcelona
en España (en es-pan-ya)	in Spain
en México (en me-hee-koe)	in Mexico
Pasamos la Navidad en México. (pass-arm-oss la na-vee-dad en me-hee-koe)	We spent Christmas in Mexico.
Pasó septiembre en España. (pass-o sep-tee-em-brey en es-pan-ya)	You spent September in Spain.
y (ee)	and
fue (fway)	it was
fue romántico (fway roe-man-tick-oh)	it was romantic
adorable (ad-or-arb-lay)	lovely / adorable
fue adorable (fway ad-or-arb-lay)	it was lovely / it was adorable
Pasé el fin de semana en Barcelona… y fue adorable. (pass-ay el fin dey sem-arn-er en bar-sair-loan-er / bar-thair-loan-er ee fway ad-or-arb-lay)	I spent the weekend in Barcelona… and it was lovely.
invitación (in-vit-ass-ee-on)	invitation
Invité (in-vit-ay)	I invited
preparación (pray-par-ass-ee-on)	preparation

Preparé (pre-par-ay)	I prepared
reservación (re-surv-ass-ee-on / re-surv-ath-ee-on)	reservation (preferred in Latin American)
reserva (re-surv-a)	reservation (preferred in Spain)
Reservé (re-surv-ay)	I reserved / booked
cooperación (cope-air-ass-ee-on / cope-air-ath-ee-on)	cooperation
Cooperé (cope-air-ay)	I cooperated
imaginación (im-a-hin-ass-ee-on / im-a-hin-ath-ee-on)	imagination
Imaginé (im-a-hin-ay)	I imagined
manipulación (man-ip-ool-ass-ee-on / man-ip-ool-ath-ee-on)	manipulation
Manipulé (man-ip-ool-ay)	I manipulated
continuación (con-tin-oo-ass-ee-on / con-tin-oo-ath-ee-on)	continuation
Continué (con-tin-oo-ay)	I continued
participación (par-tis-ip-ass-ee-on / par-tith-ip-ath-ee-on)	participation
Participé (par-tis-ip-ay / par-tith-ip-ay)	I participated
exageración (ex-a-hair-ass-ee-on / ex-a-hair-ath-ee-on)	exaggeration
Exageré (ex-a-hair-ay)	I exaggerated
admiración (ad-mi-rass-ee-on / ad-mi-rath-ee-on)	admiration
Admiré (ad-mi-ray)	I admired
irritación (ee-ri-tass-ee-on / ee-ri-tath-ee-on)	irritation
Irrité (ee-ri-tay)	I irritated
conversación (con-vair-sass-ee-on / con-vair-sath-ee-on)	conversation
Conversé (con-vair-say)	I conversed
Ordené (or-den-ay)	I ordered (preferred in Latin American)

Pedí (pe-dee)	I ordered (literally "I asked for") – (preferred in Spain)
Pagué (pag-ay)	I paid
Hice (ee-say / ee-thay)	I did
la cuenta (la kwen-ta)	the bill
la cena (la say-ner / thay-ner)	the dinner
sopa (soap-er)	soup
una mesa (oon-er may-ser)	a table
una habitación (oon-er ab-it-ass-ee-on / ab-it-ath-ee-on)	a room
un taxi (oon taxi)	a taxi
Preparé la cena. (pre-par-ay la say-ner / thay-ner)	I prepared the dinner.
Ordené sopa para la cena. (or-den-ay soap-er pa-ra la say-ner / thay-ner)	I ordered soup for dinner. (preferred in Latin American)
Pedí sopa para la cena. (pe-dee soap-er pa-ra la say-ner / thay-ner)	I ordered soup for dinner. (preferred in Spain)
Reservé una mesa para usted. (re-surv-ay oon-er may-ser pa-ra oo-sted)	I booked a table for you.
Ella reservó (ay-a re-surv-o)	She booked / reserved
Ella reservó una mesa para esta noche. (ay-a re-surv-ay oon-er may-ser pa-ra es-ta noch-ay)	She booked / reserved a table for this evening.
Él reservó (el re-surv-o)	He booked / reserved
Él reservó una habitación para dos personas. (el re-surv-o oon-er ab-it-ass-ee-on / ab-it-ath-ee-on pa-ra doss pair-so-nass)	He booked / reserved a room for two people.
¿Qué? (kay)	What?
¿Qué preparó? (kay pre-par-o)	What did you prepare?
¿Qué preparó usted? (kay pre-par-o oo-sted)	What did you prepare?
¿Qué hizo usted? (kay ee-soe / ee-thoe oo-sted)	What did you do?

Reservé una mesa, ordené la cena y luego pagué la cuenta. ¿Qué hizo usted? (re-surv-ay oon-er may-ser, or-den-ay la say-ner / thay-ner ee loo-way-go pag-ay la kwen-ta. kay ee-soe / ee-thoe oo-sted)	I booked a table, ordered dinner and then paid the bill. What did you do?
Tengo la intención de… (ten-go la in-ten-see-on / in-ten-thee-on dey)	I'm planning to… (literally "I have the intention of…")
Tengo la intención de volver a España en mayo. (ten-go la in-ten-see-on / in-ten-thee-on dey vol-vair a es-pan-ya en my-oh)	I'm planning to go back to Spain in May.
Tengo miedo de… (ten-go mee-ed-oh dey)	I'm scared of… (literally "I have fear of…")
Tengo miedo de volver a España en septiembre. (ten-go mee-ed-oh dey vol-vair a es-pan-ya en sep-tee-em-brey)	I'm scared of going back to Spain in September.
¿De verdad? (dey vair-dad)	Really?
por lo que (poor-low-kay)	so
pero (pair-o)	but
Tengo ganas de… (ten-go ga-nas dey)	I feel like… / I fancy… (literally "I have desire of…")
Sí, tengo ganas de volver a Barcelona, pero tengo miedo de volar, por lo que tengo la intención de tomar el Eurostar. (see ten-go ga-nas dey vol-vair a bar-sair-loan-er / bar-thair-loan-er pair-o ten-go mee-ed-oh dey vol-ar, poor-low-kay ten-go la in-ten-see-on / in-ten-thee-on dey to-mar el e-oo-roe-star)	Yes, I feel like going back to Barcelona but I'm scared of flying, so I'm planning to take the Eurostar.
Tengo ganas de comprar algo esta mañana. (ten-go ga-nas dey com-prar al-go es-ta man-yarn-a)	I feel like / fancy buying something this morning.
Tengo ganas de leer algo esta tarde. (ten-go ga-nas dey lay-air al-go es-ta tar-dey)	I feel like / fancy reading something this afternoon.

Tiene (tee-en-ey)	You have (formal)
Tiene ganas de comer algo esta noche. (tee-en-ey ga-nas dey kom-air al-go)	You feel like eating something this evening. (formal)
Necesito (ness-e-seet-oh / neth-e-seet-oh)	I need
Necesito hablar español. (ness-e-seet-oh / neth-e-seet-oh a-blar es-pa-nyol)	I need to speak Spanish.
Necesito un taxi. (ness-e-seet-oh / neth-e-seet-oh oon taxi)	I need a taxi.
Necesito una habitación. (ness-e-seet-oh / neth-e-seet-oh oon-er ab-it-ass-ee-on / ab-it-ath-ee-on)	I need a room.
Necesito ayuda. (ness-e-seet-oh / neth-e-seet-oh a-yoo-der)	I need help.
¡Necesitas ayuda, camarada! (ness-e-seet-ass / neth-e-seet-ass a-yoo-der ca-ma-ra-da)	You need help, mate!
Odio (oh-dee-oh)	I hate
¡Odio volar! (oh-dee-oh vol-ar)	I hate flying!
Odio vivir con mis suegros. (odio viv-eer kon miss soo-egg-ros)	I hate living with my in-laws.
Odias comer con mis padres. (oh-dee-ass kom-air kon miss pard-res)	You hate eating with my parents. (informal)
Odia trabajar aquí. (oh-dee-a trab-a-har a-key)	You hate working here. (formal)
solitario (so-lit-ar-ee-oh)	solitary
contrario (kon-trar-ee-oh)	contrary
ordinario (or-din-ar-ee-oh)	ordinary

Now, time to do it the other way around!

the weekend	**el fin de semana** (el fin dey sem-arn-er)
romantic	**romántico** (roe-man-tick-oh)
typical	**típico** (tip-ick-oh)
political	**político** (po-li-tick-oh)
logical	**lógico** (lo-hee-koh)
historical	**histórico** (ee-sto-rick-oh)
critical	**crítico** (kri-tick-oh)
classical	**clásico** (clas-ick-oh)
electrical	**eléctrico** (el-ek-trick-oh)
identical	**idéntico** (ee-dent-ick-oh)
biological	**biológico** (bee-oh-lo-hee-koh)
I visited	**Visité** (visit-ay)
Barcelona	**Barcelona** (bar-sair-loan-er / bar-thair-loan-er)
Madrid	**Madrid** (ma-drid)
I visited Madrid.	**Visité Madrid.** (visit-ay ma-drid)
I spent	**Pasé** (pass-ay)
You spent	**Pasó** (pass-o)
We spent	**Pasamos** (pass-arm-oss)
September	**septiembre** (sep-tee-em-brey)
Christmas (literally "the Christmas")	**la Navidad** (la na-vee-dad)
in Barcelona	**en Barcelona** (en bar-sair-loan-er / bar-thair-loan-er)
in Spain	**en España** (en es-pan-ya)
in Mexico	**en México** (en me-hee-koe)
We spent Christmas in Mexico.	**Pasamos la Navidad en México.** (pass-arm-oss la na-vee-dad en me-hee-koe)
You spent September in Spain.	**Pasó septiembre en España.** (pass-o sep-tee-em-brey en es-pan-ya)

and	**y** (ee)
it was	**fue** (fway)
it was romantic	**fue romántico** (fway roe-man-tick-oh)
lovely / adorable	**adorable** (ad-or-arb-lay)
it was lovely / it was adorable	**fue adorable** (fway ad-or-arb-lay)
I spent the weekend in Barcelona… and it was lovely.	**Pasé el fin de semana en Barcelona… y fue adorable.** (pass-ay el fin dey sem-arn-er en bar-sair-loan-er / bar-thair-loan-er ee fway ad-or-arb-lay)
invitation	**invitación** (in-vit-ass-ee-on)
I invited	**Invité** (in-vit-ay)
preparation	**preparación** (pray-par-ass-ee-on)
I prepared	**Preparé** (pre-par-ay)
reservation (preferred in Latin American)	**reservación** (re-surv-ass-ee-on / re-surv-ath-ee-on)
reservation (preferred in Spain)	**reserva** (re-surv-a)
I reserved / booked	**Reservé** (re-surv-ay)
cooperation	**cooperación** (cope-air-ass-ee-on / cope-air-ath-ee-on)
I cooperated	**Cooperé** (cope-air-ay)
imagination	**imaginación** (im-a-hin-ass-ee-on / im-a-hin-ath-ee-on)
I imagined	**Imaginé** (im-a-hin-ay)
manipulation	**manipulación** (man-ip-ool-ass-ee-on / man-ip-ool-ath-ee-on)
I manipulated	**Manipulé** (man-ip-ool-ay)
continuation	**continuación** (con-tin-oo-ass-ee-on / con-tin-oo-ath-ee-on)
I continued	**Continué** (con-tin-oo-ay)
participation	**participación** (par-tis-ip-ass-ee-on / par-tith-ip-ath-ee-on)
I participated	**Participé** (par-tis-ip-ay / par-tith-ip-ay)

exaggeration	exageración (ex-a-hair-ass-ee-on / ex-a-hair-ath-ee-on)
I exaggerated	Exageré (ex-a-hair-ay)
admiration	admiración (ad-mi-rass-ee-on / ad-mi-rath-ee-on)
I admired	Admiré (ad-mi-ray)
irritation	irritación (ee-ri-tass-ee-on / ee-ri-tath-ee-on)
I irritated	Irrité (ee-ri-tay)
conversation	conversación (con-vair-sass-ee-on / con-vair-sath-ee-on)
I conversed	Conversé (con-vair-say)
I ordered (preferred in Latin American)	Ordené (or-den-ay)
I ordered (literally "I asked for") – (preferred in Spain)	Pedí (pe-dee)
I paid	Pagué (pag-ay)
I did	Hice (ee-say / ee-thay)
the bill	la cuenta (la kwen-ta)
the dinner	la cena (la say-ner / thay-ner)
soup	sopa (soap-er)
a table	una mesa (oon-er may-ser)
a room	una habitación (oon-er ab-it-ass-ee-on / ab-it-ath-ee-on)
a taxi	un taxi (oon taxi)
I prepared the dinner.	Preparé la cena. (pre-par-ay la say-ner / thay-ner)
I ordered soup for dinner. (preferred in Latin American)	Ordené sopa para la cena. (or-den-ay soap-er pa-ra la say-ner / thay-ner)
I ordered soup for dinner. (preferred in Spain)	Pedí sopa para la cena. (pe-dee soap-er pa-ra la say-ner / thay-ner)
I booked a table for you.	Reservé una mesa para usted. (re-surv-ay oon-er may-ser pa-ra oo-stedd)
She booked / reserved	Ella reservó (ay-a re-surv-o)

She booked / reserved a table for this evening.	Ella reservó una mesa para esta noche. (ay-a re-surv-ay oon-er may-ser pa-ra es-ta noch-ay)
He booked / reserved	Él reservó (el re-surv-o)
He booked / reserved a room for two people.	Él reservó una habitación para dos personas. (el re-surv-o oon-er ab-it-ass-ee-on / ab-it-ath-ee-on pa-ra doss pair-so-nass)
What?	¿Qué? (kay)
What did you prepare?	¿Qué preparó? (kay pre-par-o)
What did you prepare?	¿Qué preparó usted? (kay pre-par-o oo-sted)
What did you do?	¿Qué hizo usted? (kay ee-soe / ee-thoe oo-sted)
I booked a table, ordered dinner and then paid the bill. What did you do?	Reservé una mesa, ordené la cena y luego pagué la cuenta. ¿Qué hizo usted? (re-surv-ay oon-er may-ser, or-den-ay la say-ner / thay-ner ee loo-way-go pag-ay la kwen-ta. kay ee-soe / ee-thoe oo-sted)
I'm planning to… (literally "I have the intention of…")	Tengo la intención de… (ten-go la in-ten-see-on / in-ten-thee-on dey)
I'm planning to go back to Spain in May.	Tengo la intención de volver a España en mayo. (ten-go la in-ten-see-on / in-ten-thee-on dey vol-vair a es-pan-ya en my-oh)
I'm scared of… (literally "I have fear of…")	Tengo miedo de… (ten-go mee-ed-oh dey)
I'm scared of going back to Spain in September.	Tengo miedo de volver a España en septiembre. (ten-go mee-ed-oh dey vol-vair a es-pan-ya en sep-tee-em-brey)
Really?	¿De verdad? (dey vair-dad)
so	por lo que (poor-low-kay)
but	pero (pair-o)
I feel like… / I fancy… (literally "I have desire of…")	Tengo ganas de… (ten-go ga-nas dey)

Yes, I feel like going back to Barcelona but I'm scared of flying, so I'm planning to take the Eurostar.	Sí, tengo ganas de volver a Barcelona, pero tengo miedo de volar, por lo que tengo la intención de tomar el Eurostar. (see ten-go ga-nas dey vol-vair a bar-sair-loan-er / bar-thair-loan-er pair-o ten-go mee-ed-oh dey vol-ar, poor-low-kay ten-go la in-ten-see-on / in-ten-thee-on dey to-mar el e-oo-roe-star)
I feel like / fancy buying something this morning.	Tengo ganas de comprar algo esta mañana. (ten-go ga-nas dey com-prar al-go es-ta man-yarn-a)
I feel like / fancy reading something this afternoon.	Tengo ganas de leer algo esta tarde. (ten-go ga-nas dey lay-air al-go es-ta tar-dey)
You have (formal)	Tiene (tee-en-ey)
You feel like eating something this evening. (formal)	Tiene ganas de comer algo esta noche. (tee-en-ey ga-nas dey kom-air al-go)
I need	Necesito (ness-e-seet-oh / neth-e-seet-oh)
I need to speak Spanish.	Necesito hablar español. (ness-e-seet-oh / neth-e-seet-oh a-blar es-pa-nyol)
I need a taxi.	Necesito un taxi. (ness-e-seet-oh / neth-e-seet-oh oon taxi)
I need a room.	Necesito una habitación. (ness-e-seet-oh / neth-e-seet-oh oon-er ab-it-ass-ee-on / ab-it-ath-ee-on)
I need help.	Necesito ayuda. (ness-e-seet-oh / neth-e-seet-oh a-yoo-der)
You need help, mate!	¡Necesitas ayuda, camarada! (ness-e-seet-ass / neth-e-seet-ass a-yoo-der ca-ma-ra-da)
I hate	Odio (oh-dee-oh)
I hate flying!	¡Odio volar! (oh-dee-oh vol-ar)

I hate living with my in-laws.	**Odio vivir con mis suegros.** (odio viv-eer kon miss soo-egg-ros)
You hate eating with my parents. (informal)	**Odias comer con mis padres.** (oh-dee-ass kom-air kon miss pard-res)
You hate working here. (formal)	**Odia trabajar aquí.** (oh-dee-a trab-a-har a-key)
solitary	**solitario** (so-lit-ar-ee-oh)
contrary	**contrario** (kon-trar-ee-oh)
ordinary	**ordinario** (or-din-ar-ee-oh)

Well, that's it, you're done with Chapter 4! Remember, don't try to hold onto or remember anything you've learnt here. Everything you learnt in earlier chapters will be brought back up and reinforced in later chapters. You don't need to do anything or make any effort to memorise anything.

Between Chapters Tip!

Use your "hidden moments"

A famous American linguist, Barry Farber, learnt a large part of the languages he spoke during the "hidden moments" he found in everyday life. Such hidden moments might include the time he would spend waiting for a train to arrive, or time spent waiting for the kids to come out of school, or for the traffic to get moving in the morning. These "hidden moments" would otherwise have been useless and unimportant in his daily life but, for someone learning a language, they can be some of the most useful minutes of the day.

Breaking up your studies into lots of little bits like this can also be useful as a way to help stop them from feeling like a great effort, or from becoming impractical when your life gets especially hectic.

So, keep this book in your pocket whenever you go out and then make use of such "hidden moments" whenever they come along!

CHAPTER 5

I was just about to book
a taxi when you called me.

I was just about to book a taxi when you called me.

Well, here we are again.

Another chapter, beginning with another simple sentence:

"I was just about to book a taxi when you called me." This sentence has some very useful stuff in it, but as before, even if you know some Spanish already, you may still struggle with a sentence that seems basic in English but that requires just a bit of guidance to construct in Spanish.

Okay, let's go!

"I was" in Spanish is:

Estaba
(es-tah-bah)

And if you want to say "I was about to..." or "I was just about to..." in Spanish, you will literally say "I was at point of...", which is:

Estaba a punto de...
(es-tah-bah a poon-toe dey)

Now, what is "to reserve" or "to book" in Spanish?

reservar
(re-surv-ar)

And what would be "to book a table"?

reservar una mesa
(re-surv-ar oon-er may-ser)

And again, what was "I was about to…" / "I was just about to…" (literally "I was at point of…")?

Estaba a punto de…
(es-tah-bah a poon-toe dey)

So, how would you say "I was about to book a table" (literally "I was at point of to book a table")?

Estaba a punto de reservar una mesa.
(es-tah-bah a poon-toe dey re-surv-ar oon-er may-ser)

What about "I was about to book a taxi"?

Estaba a punto de reservar un taxi.
(es-tah-bah a poon-toe dey re-surv-ar oon taxi)

"To prepare" in Spanish is:

preparar
(pre-par-ar)

So what would be "to prepare the dinner"?

preparar la cena
(pre-par-ar la say-ner / thay-ner)

And how would you say "I was about to prepare the dinner"?

Estaba a punto de preparar la cena.
(es-tah-bah a poon-toe dey pre-par-ar la say-ner / thay-ner)

"To pay" is:

pagar
(pag-ar)

So, how would you say "to pay the bill"?

pagar la cuenta
pag-ar la kwen-ta

117

Now, try to say "I was about to pay the bill" (literally "I was at point of to pay the bill").

Estaba a punto de pagar la cuenta.
(es-tah-bah a poon-toe dey pag-ar la kwen-ta)

And once more, how would you say "I was about to book a taxi"?

Estaba a punto de reservar un taxi.
(es-tah-bah a poon-toe dey re-surv-ar oon taxi)

And "I was about to book a table"?

Estaba a punto de reservar una mesa.
(es-tah-bah a poon-toe dey re-surv-ar oon-er may-ser)

Again, how would you say "I was about to prepare the dinner"?

Estaba a punto de preparar la cena.
(es-tah-bah a poon-toe dey pre-par-ar la say-ner / thay-ner)

"You called" (informal) in Spanish is:

llamaste
(yah-mah-stay)

To say "you called me" (informal) in Spanish, you literally say "me you called":

me llamaste
(may yah-mah-stay)

The word for "when" in Spanish is:

cuando
(kwan-doh)

So, how would you say "...when you called me" (informal) – (literally "...when you me called")?

...cuando me llamaste
(kwan-doh may yah-mah-stay)

Now once again, how would you say "I was about to prepare the dinner"?

Estaba a punto de preparar la cena.
(es-tah-bah a poon-toe dey pre-par-ar la say-ner / thay-ner)

Let's put these two parts together and say "I was about to prepare the dinner when you called me."

Estaba a punto de preparar la cena cuando me llamaste.
(es-tah-bah a poon-toe dey pre-par-ar la say-ner / thay-ner kwan-doh may yah-mah-stay)

How about "I was about to book a table when you called me"?

Estaba a punto de reservar una mesa cuando me llamaste.
(es-tah-bah a poon-toe dey re-surv-ar oon-er may-sar kwan-doh may yah-mah-stay)

And again, how would you say "I was about to pay the bill"?

Estaba a punto de pagar la cuenta.
(es-tah-bah a poon-toe dey pag-ar la kwen-ta)

So how would you say "I was about to pay the bill when you called me"?

Estaba a punto de pagar la cuenta cuando me llamaste.
(es-tah-bah a poon-toe dey pag-ar la kwen-ta kwan-doh may yah-mah-stay)

And finally, going back to the title of this chapter, how would you say "I was about to book a taxi when you called me"?

Estaba a punto de reservar un taxi cuando me llamaste.
(es-tah-bah a poon-toe dey re-surv-ar oon taxi kwan-doh may yah-mah-stay)

Well that wasn't too hard, was it? Another excellent sentence complete!

Building Blocks 5

Here they are:

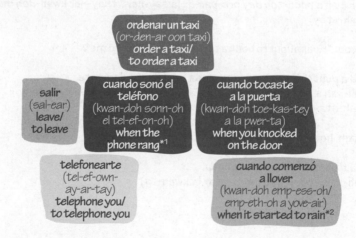

*1 literally "when sounded the telephone"

*2 literally "commenced"

You know what to do!

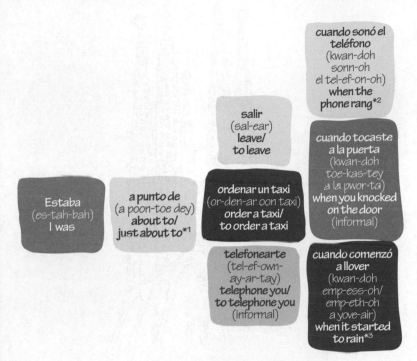

cuando sonó el teléfono
(kwan-doh
sonn-oh
el tel-ef-on-oh)
when the phone rang*2

salir
(sal-ear)
**leave/
to leave**

**cuando tocaste
a la puerta**
(kwan-doh
toe-kas-tey
a la pwor-ta)
**when you knocked
on the door**
(informal)

Estaba
(es-tah-bah)
I was

a punto de
(a poon-toe dey)
**about to/
just about to***1

ordenar un taxi
(or-den-ar oon taxi)
**order a taxi/
to order a taxi**

telefonearte
(tel-ef-own-
ay-ar-tay)
**telephone you/
to telephone you**
(informal)

**cuando comenzó
a llover**
(kwan-doh
emp-ess-oh/
emp-eth-oh
a yove-air)
**when it started
to rain***3

*1 literally "at point of"

*2 literally "when sounded the telephone"

*3 literally "commenced"

You know what to do!

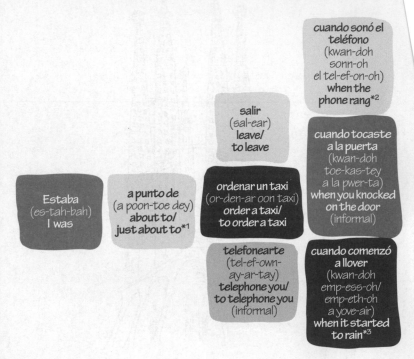

cuando sonó el
teléfono
(kwan-doh
sonn-oh
el tel-ef-on-oh)
when the
phone rang*2

salir
(sal-ear)
leave/
to leave

cuando tocaste
a la puerta
(kwan-doh
toe-kas-tey
a la pwer-ta)
when you knocked
on the door
(informal)

Estaba
(es-tah-bah)
I was

a punto de
(a poon-toe dey)
about to/
just about to*1

ordenar un taxi
(or-den-ar oon taxi)
order a taxi/
to order a taxi

telefonearte
(tel-ef-own-
ay-ar-tay)
telephone you/
to telephone you
(informal)

cuando comenzó
a llover
(kwan-doh
emp-ess-oh/
emp-eth-oh
a yove-air)
when it started
to rain*3

*1 literally "at point of"

*2 literally "when sounded the telephone"

*3 literally "commenced"

histórico (ee-sto-rick-oh)	historical
crítico (kri-tick-oh)	critical
clásico (clas-ick-oh)	classical
eléctrico (el-ek-trick-oh)	electrical
idéntico (ee-dent-ick-oh)	identical
biológico (bee-oh-lo-hee-koh)	biological
entusiasmado (en-tooz-ee-as-mard-oh)	enthusiastic[10]
Visité (visit-ay)	I visited
Barcelona (bar-sair-loan-er / bar-thair-loan-er)	Barcelona
Madrid (ma-drid)	Madrid
Visité Madrid. (visit-ay ma-drid)	I visited Madrid.
Pasé (pass-ay)	I spent
Pasó (pass-o)	You spent
Pasamos (pass-arm-oss)	We spent
septiembre (sep-tee-em-brey)	September
la Navidad (la na-vee-dad)	Christmas (literally "the Christmas")
en Barcelona (en bar-sair-loan-er / bar-thair-loan-er)	in Barcelona
en España (en es-pan-ya)	in Spain
en México (en me-hee-koe)	in Mexico
Pasamos la Navidad en México. (pass-arm-oss la na-vee-dad en me-hee-koe)	We spent Christmas in Mexico.

---

10 In everything in life you will find exceptions to the rule and the same is true with these wonderful "ic" and "ical" word robberies. Although these conversions work almost all the time, "enthusiastic" is an exception to this technique that I would like you to learn. It's still an easy word to pick up, as it is similar to the English, but it does not change in the way you would expect it to. I will leave it in the checklists from now on so that you learn it well.

Pasó septiembre en España. (pass-o sep-tee-em-brey en es-pan-ya)	You spent September in Spain.
y (ee)	and
fue (fway)	it was
fue romántico (fway roe-man-tick-oh)	it was romantic
adorable (ad-or-arb-lay)	lovely / adorable
fue adorable (fway ad-or-arb-lay)	it was lovely / it was adorable
Pasé el fin de semana en Barcelona… y fue adorable. (pass-ay el fin dey sem-arn-er en bar-sair-loan-er / bar-thair-loan-er ee fway ad-or-arb-lay)	I spent the weekend in Barcelona… and it was lovely.
invitación (in-vit-ass-ee-on)	invitation
Invité (in-vit-ay)	I invited
preparación (pray-par-ass-ee-on)	preparation
Preparé (pre-par-ay)	I prepared
reservación (re-surv-ass-ee-on / re-surv-ath-ee-on)	reservation (preferred in Latin American)
reserva (re-surv-a)	reservation (preferred in Spain)
Reservé (re-surv-ay)	I reserved / booked
cooperación (cope-air-ass-ee-on / cope-air-ath-ee-on)	cooperation
Cooperé (cope-air-ay)	I cooperated
imaginación (im-a-hin-ass-ee-on / im-a-hin-ath-ee-on)	imagination
Imaginé (im-a-hin-ay)	I imagined
manipulación (man-ip-ool-ass-ee-on / man-ip-ool-ath-ee-on)	manipulation
Manipulé (man-ip-ool-ay)	I manipulated
continuación (con-tin-oo-ass-ee-on / con-tin-oo-ath-ee-on)	continuation

Continué (con-tin-oo-ay)	I continued
participación (par-tis-ip-ass-ee-on / par-tith-ip-ath-ee-on)	participation
Participé (par-tis-ip-ay / par-tith-ip-ay)	I participated
exageración (ex-a-hair-ass-ee-on / ex-a-hair-ath-ee-on)	exaggeration
Exageré (ex-a-hair-ay)	I exaggerated
admiración (ad-mi-rass-ee-on / ad-mi-rath-ee-on)	admiration
Admiré (ad-mi-ray)	I admired
irritación (ee-ri-tass-ee-on / ee-ri-tath-ee-on)	irritation
Irrité (ee-ri-tay)	I irritated
conversación (con-vair-sass-ee-on / con-vair-sath-ee-on)	conversation
Conversé (con-vair-say)	I conversed
Ordené (or-den-ay)	I ordered (preferred in Latin American)
Pedí (pe-dee)	I ordered (literally "I asked for") – (preferred in Spain)
Pagué (pag ay)	I paid
Hice (ee-say / ee-thay)	I did
la cuenta (la kwen-ta)	the bill
la cena (la say-ner / thay-ner)	the dinner
sopa (soap-er)	soup
una mesa (oon-er may-ser)	a table
una habitación (oon-er ab-it-ass-ee-on / ab-it-ath-ee-on)	a room
un taxi (oon taxi)	a taxi
Preparé la cena. (pre-par-ay la say-ner / thay-ner)	I prepared the dinner.
Ordené sopa para la cena. (or-den-ay soap-er pa-ra la say-ner / thay-ner)	I ordered soup for dinner. (preferred in Latin American)

Pedí sopa para la cena. (pe-dee soap-er pa-ra la say-ner / thay-ner)	I ordered soup for dinner. (preferred in Spain)
Reservé una mesa para usted. (re-surv-ay oon-er may-ser pa-ra oo-stedd)	I booked a table for you.
Ella reservó (ay-a re-surv-o)	She booked / reserved
Ella reservó una mesa para esta noche. (ay-a re-surv-ay oon-er may-ser pa-ra es-ta noch-ay)	She booked / reserved a table for this evening.
Él reservó (el re-surv-o)	He booked / reserved
Él reservó una habitación para dos personas. (el re-surv-o oon-er ab-it-ass-ee-on / ab-it-ath-ee-on pa-ra doss pair-so-nass)	He booked / reserved a room for two people.
¿Qué? (kay)	What?
¿Qué preparó? (kay pre-par-o)	What did you prepare?
¿Qué preparó usted? (kay pre-par-o oo-sted)	What did you prepare?
¿Qué hizo usted? (kay ee-soe / ee-thoe oo-sted)	What did you do?
Reservé una mesa, ordené la cena y luego pagué la cuenta. ¿Qué hizo usted? (re-surv-ay oon-er may-ser, or-den-ay la say-ner / thay-ner ee loo-way-go pag-ay la kwen-ta. kay ee-soe / ee-thoe oo-sted)	I booked a table, ordered dinner and then paid the bill. What did you do?
Tengo la intención de... (ten-go la in-ten-see-on / in-ten-thee-on dey)	I'm planning to... (literally "I have the intention of...")
Tengo la intención de volver a España en mayo. (ten-go la in-ten-see-on / in-ten-thee-on dey vol-vair a es-pan-ya en my-oh)	I'm planning to go back to Spain in May.
Tengo miedo de... (ten-go mee-ed-oh dey)	I'm scared of... (literally "I have fear of...")
Tengo miedo de volver a España en septiembre. (ten-go mee-ed-oh dey vol-vair a es-pan-ya en sep-tee-em-brey)	I'm scared of going back to Spain in September.

¿De verdad? (dey vair-dad)	Really?
por lo que (poor-low-kay)	so
pero (pair-o)	but
Tengo ganas de... (ten-go ga-nas dey)	I feel like... / I fancy... (literally "I have desire of...")
Sí, tengo ganas de volver a Barcelona, pero tengo miedo de volar, por lo que tengo la intención de tomar el Eurostar. (see ten-go ga-nas dey vol-vair a bar-sair-loan-er / bar-thair-loan-er pair o ten go mee-ed-oh dey vol-ar, poor-low-kay ten-go la in-ten-see-on / in-ten-thee-on dey to-mar el e-oo-roe-star)	Yes, I feel like going back to Barcelona but I'm scared of flying, so I'm planning to take the Eurostar.
Tengo ganas de comprar algo esta mañana. (ten-go ga-nas dey com-prar al-go es-ta man yarn a)	I feel like / fancy buying something this morning.
Tengo ganas de leer algo esta tarde. (ten-go ga-nas dey lay-air al-go es-ta tar-dey)	I feel like / fancy reading something this afternoon.
Tiene (tee-en-ey)	You have (formal)
Tiene ganas de comer algo esta noche. (tee-en-ey ga-nas dey kom-air al-go)	You feel like eating something this evening. (formal)
Necesito (ness-e-seet-oh / noth-e-seet-oh)	I need
Necesito hablar español. (ness-e-seet-oh / neth-e-seet-oh a-blar es-pa-nyol)	I need to speak Spanish.
Necesito un taxi. (ness-e-seet-oh / neth-e-seet-oh oon taxi)	I need a taxi.
Necesito una habitación. (ness-e-seet-oh / neth-e-seet-oh oon-er ab-it-ass-ee-on / ab-it-ath-ee-on)	I need a room.

Necesito ayuda. (ness-e-seet-oh / neth-e-seet-oh a-yoo-der)	I need help.
¡Necesitas ayuda, camarada! (ness-e-seet-ass / neth-e-seet-ass a-yoo-der ca-ma-ra-da)	You need help, mate!
Odio (oh-dee-oh)	I hate
¡Odio volar! (oh-dee-oh vol-ar)	I hate flying!
Odio vivir con mis suegros. (odio viv-eer kon miss soo-egg-ros)	I hate living with my in-laws.
Odias comer con mis padres. (oh-dee-ass kom-air kon miss pard-res)	You hate eating with my parents. (informal)
Odia trabajar aquí. (oh-dee-a trab-a-har a-key)	You hate working here. (formal)
Estaba (es-tah-bah)	I was
solitario (so-lit-ar-ee-oh)	solitary
contrario (kon-trar-ee-oh)	contrary
ordinario (or-din-ar-ee-oh)	ordinary
Estaba a punto de… (es-tah-bah a poon-toe dey)	I was about to… / I was just about to… (literally "I was at point of…")
Estaba a punto de preparar la cena. (es-tah-bah a poon-toe dey pre-par-ar la say-ner / thay-ner)	I was about to prepare the dinner / I was just about to prepare the dinner.
Estaba a punto de pagar la cuenta. (es-tah-bah a poon-toe dey pag-ar la kwen-ta)	I was about to pay the bill.[11]
Estaba a punto de reservar una mesa. (es-tah-bah a poon-toe dey re-surv-ar oon-er may-ser)	I was just about to book a table.
Me llamaste. (may yah-mah-stay)	You called me / You did call me / You have called me. (informal)
cuando (kwan-doh)	when

---

11   All of the "about to…" sentences here can be translated as "I was about to…" or "I was *just* about to…". Sometimes only one translation is given but, in all cases, you could translate it either way.

Estaba a punto de reservar un taxi cuando me llamaste. (es-tah-bah a poon-toe dey re-surv-ar oon taxi kwan-doh may yah-mah-stay.)	I was just about to book a taxi when you called me.
Estaba a punto de salir cuando sonó el teléfono. (es-tah-bah a poon-toe dey sal-ear kwan-doh sonn-oh el tel-ef-on-oh)	I was about to leave when the telephone rang.
Estaba a punto de telefonearte cuando tocaste a la puerta. (es-tah-bah a poon-toe dey tel-ef-own-ay-ar-tay kwan-doh toe-kas-tey a la pwer-ta)	I was just about to phone you when you knocked at the door. (informal)
Estaba a punto de reservar un taxi cuando comenzó a llover. (es-tah-bah a poon-toe dey re-surv-ar oon taxi kwan-doh emp-ess-oh / emp-eth-oh a yove-air)	I was just about to order a taxi when it started (literally "commenced") to rain.

Okay, time for the other way around. Isn't it strange how translating Spanish into English is much easier than translating English into Spanish...?

the weekend	**el fin de semana** (el fin dey sem-arn-er)
romantic	**romántico** (roe-man-tick-oh)
typical	**típico** (tip-ick-oh)
political	**político** (po-li-tick-oh)
logical	**lógico** (lo-hee-koh)
historical	**histórico** (ee-sto-rick-oh)
critical	**crítico** (kri-tick-oh)
classical	**clásico** (clas-ick-oh)
electrical	**eléctrico** (el-ek-trick-oh)
identical	**idéntico** (ee-dent-ick-oh)

biological	biológico (bee-oh-lo-hee-koh)
enthusiastic	entusiasmado (en-tooz-ee-as-mard-oh)
I visited	Visité (visit-ay)
Barcelona	Barcelona (bar-sair-loan-er / bar-thair-loan-er)
Madrid	Madrid (ma-drid)
I visited Madrid.	Visité Madrid. (visit-ay ma-drid)
I spent	Pasé (pass-ay)
You spent	Pasó (pass-o)
We spent	Pasamos (pass-arm-oss)
September	septiembre (sep-tee-em-brey)
Christmas (literally "the Christmas")	la Navidad (la na-vee-dad)
in Barcelona	en Barcelona (en bar-sair-loan-er / bar-thair-loan-er)
in Spain	en España (en es-pan-ya)
in Mexico	en México (en me-hee-koe)
We spent Christmas in Mexico.	Pasamos la Navidad en México. (pass-arm-oss la na-vee-dad en me-hee-koe)
You spent September in Spain.	Pasó septiembre en España. (pass-o sep-tee-em-brey en es-pan-ya)
and	y (ee)
it was	fue (fway)
it was romantic	fue romántico (fway roe-man-tick-oh)
lovely / adorable	adorable (ad-or-arb-lay)
it was lovely / it was adorable	fue adorable (fway ad-or-arb-lay)

I spent the weekend in Barcelona… and it was lovely.	Pasé el fin de semana en Barcelona… y fue adorable. (pass-ay el fin dey sem-arn-er en bar-sair-loan-er / bar-thair-loan-er ee fway ad-or-arb-lay)
invitation	invitación (in-vit-ass-ee-on)
I invited	Invité (in-vit-ay)
preparation	preparación (pray-par-ass-ee-on)
I prepared	Preparé (pre-par-ay)
reservation (preferred in Latin American)	reservación (re-surv-ass-ee-on / re-surv-ath-ee-on)
reservation (preferred in Spain)	reserva (re-surv-a)
I reserved / booked	Reservé (re-surv-ay)
cooperation	cooperación (cope-air-ass-ee-on / cope-air-ath-ee-on)
I cooperated	Cooperé (cope-air-ay)
imagination	imaginación (im-a-hin-ass-ee-on / im-a-hin-ath-ee-on)
I imagined	Imaginé (im-a-hin-ay)
manipulation	manipulación (man-ip-ool-ass-ee-on / man-ip-ool-ath-ee-on)
I manipulated	Manipulé (man-ip-ool-ay)
continuation	continuación (con-tin-oo-ass-ee-on / con-tin-oo-ath-ee-on)
I continued	Continué (con-tin-oo-ay)
participation	participación (par-tis-ip-ass-ee-on / par-tith-ip-ath-ee-on)
I participated	Participé (par-tis-ip-ay / par-tith-ip-ay)
exaggeration	exageración (ex-a-hair-ass-ee-on / ex-a-hair-ath-ee-on)
I exaggerated	Exageré (ex-a-hair-ay)

admiration	admiración (ad-mi-rass-ee-on / ad-mi-rath-ee-on)
I admired	Admiré (ad-mi-ray)
irritation	irritación (ee-ri-tass-ee-on / ee-ri-tath-ee-on)
I irritated	Irrité (ee-ri-tay)
conversation	conversación (con-vair-sass-ee-on / con-vair-sath-ee-on)
I conversed	Conversé (con-vair-say)
I ordered (preferred in Latin American)	Ordené (or-den-ay)
I ordered (literally "I asked for") – (preferred in Spain)	Pedí (pe-dee)
I paid	Pagué (pag-ay)
I did	Hice (ee-say / ee-thay)
the bill	la cuenta (la kwen-ta)
the dinner	la cena (la say-ner / thay-ner)
soup	sopa (soap-er)
a table	una mesa (oon-er may-ser)
a room	una habitación (oon-er ab-it-ass-ee-on / ab-it-ath-ee-on)
a taxi	un taxi (oon taxi)
I prepared the dinner.	Preparé la cena. (pre-par-ay la say-ner / thay-ner)
I ordered soup for dinner. (preferred in Latin American)	Ordené sopa para la cena. (or-den-ay soap-er pa-ra la say-ner / thay-ner)
I ordered soup for dinner. (preferred in Spain)	Pedí sopa para la cena. (pe-dee soap-er pa-ra la say-ner / thay-ner)
I booked a table for you.	Reservé una mesa para usted. (re-surv-ay oon-er may-ser pa-ra oo-stedd)
She booked / reserved	Ella reservó (ay-a re-surv-o)

She booked / reserved a table for this evening.	Ella reservó una mesa para esta noche. (ay-a re-surv-ay oon-er may-ser pa-ra es-ta noch-ay)
He booked / reserved	Él reservó (el re-surv-o)
He booked / reserved a room for two people.	Él reservó una habitación para dos personas. (el re-surv-o oon-er ab-it-ass-ee-on / ab-it-ath-ee-on pa-ra doss pair-so-nass)
What?	¿Qué? (kay)
What did you prepare?	¿Qué preparó? (kay pre-par-o)
What did you prepare?	¿Qué preparó usted? (kay pre-par-o oo-sted)
What did you do?	¿Qué hizo usted? (kay ee-soe / ee-thoe oo-sted)
I booked a table, ordered dinner and then paid the bill. What did you do?	Reservé una mesa, ordené la cena y luego pagué la cuenta. ¿Qué hizo usted? (re-surv-ay oon-er may-ser, or-den-ay la say-ner / thay-ner ee loo-way-go pag-ay la kwen-ta. kay ee-soe / ee-thoe oo-sted)
I'm planning to... (literally "I have the intention of...")	Tengo la intención de... (ten-go la in-ten-see-on / in-ten-thee-on dey)
I'm planning to go back to Spain in May.	Tengo la intención de volver a España en mayo. (ten-go la in-ten-see-on / in-ten-thee-on dey vol-vair a es-pan-ya en my-oh)
I'm scared of... (literally "I have fear of...")	Tengo miedo de... (ten-go mee-ed-oh dey)
I'm scared of going back to Spain in September.	Tengo miedo de volver a España en septiembre. (ten-go mee-ed-oh dey vol-vair a es-pan-ya en sep-tee-em-brey)
Really?	¿De verdad? (dey vair-dad)

so	**por lo que** (poor-low-kay)
but	**pero** (pair-o)
I feel like… / I fancy… (literally "I have desire of…")	**Tengo ganas de…** (ten-go ga-nas dey)
Yes, I feel like going back to Barcelona but I'm scared of flying, so I'm planning to take the Eurostar.	**Sí, tengo ganas de volver a Barcelona, pero tengo miedo de volar, por lo que tengo la intención de tomar el Eurostar.** (see ten-go ga-nas dey vol-vair a bar-sair-loan-er / bar-thair-loan-er pair-o ten-go mee-ed-oh dey vol-ar, poor-low-kay ten-go la in-ten-see-on / in-ten-thee-on dey to-mar el e-oo-roe-star)
I feel like / fancy buying something this morning.	**Tengo ganas de comprar algo esta mañana.** (ten-go ga-nas dey com-prar al-go es-ta man-yarn-a)
I feel like / fancy reading something this afternoon.	**Tengo ganas de leer algo esta tarde.** (ten-go ga-nas dey lay-air al-go es-ta tar-dey)
You have (formal)	**Tiene** (tee-en-ey)
You feel like eating something this evening. (formal)	**Tiene ganas de comer algo esta noche.** (tee-en-ey ga-nas dey kom-air al-go)
I need	**Necesito** (ness-e-seet-oh / neth-e-seet-oh)
I need to speak Spanish.	**Necesito hablar español.** (ness-e-seet-oh / neth-e-seet-oh a-blar es-pa-nyol)
I need a taxi.	**Necesito un taxi.** (ness-e-seet-oh / neth-e-seet-oh oon taxi)
I need a room.	**Necesito una habitación.** (ness-e-seet-oh / neth-e-seet-oh oon-er ab-it-ass-ee-on / ab-it-ath-ee-on)
I need help.	**Necesito ayuda.** (ness-e-seet-oh / neth-e-seet-oh a-yoo-der)

You need help, mate!	¡Necesitas ayuda, camarada! (ness-e-seet-ass / neth-e-seet-ass a-yoo-der ca-ma-ra-da)
I hate	Odio (oh-dee-oh)
I hate flying!	¡Odio volar! (oh-dee-oh vol-ar)
I hate living with my in-laws.	Odio vivir con mis suegros. (odio viv-eer kon miss soo-egg-ros)
You hate eating with my parents. (informal)	Odias comer con mis padres. (oh-dee-ass kom-air kon miss pard-res)
You hate working here. (formal)	Odia trabajar aquí. (oh-dee-a trab-a-har a-key)
I was	Estaba (es-tah-bah)
solitary	solitario (so-lit-ar-ee-oh)
contrary	contrario (kon-trar-ee-oh)
ordinary	ordinario (or-din-ar-ee-oh)
I was about to… / I was just about to… (literally "I was at point of…")	Estaba a punto de… (es-tah-bah a poon-toe dey)
I was about to prepare the dinner / I was just about to prepare the dinner.	Estaba a punto de preparar la cena. (es-tah-bah a poon-toe dey pre-par-ar la say-ner / thay-ner)
I was about to pay the bill.[12]	Estaba a punto de pagar la cuenta. (es-tah-bah a poon-toe dey pag-ar la kwen-ta)
I was just about to book a table.	Estaba a punto de reservar una mesa. (es-tah-bah a poon-toe dey re-surv-ar oon-er may-ser)
You called me / You did call me / You have called me. (informal)	Me llamaste. (may yah-mah-stay)
when	cuando (kwan-doh)

---

12 All of the "about to…" sentences here can be translated as "I was about to…" or "I was just about to…". Sometimes only one translation is given but, in all cases, you could translate it either way.

I was just about to book a taxi when you called me.	Estaba a punto de reservar un taxi cuando me llamaste. (es-tah-bah a poon-toe dey re-surv-ar oon taxi kwan-doh may yah-mah-stay.)
I was about to leave when the telephone rang.	Estaba a punto de salir cuando sonó el teléfono. (es-tah-bah a poon-toe dey sal-ear kwan-doh sonn-oh el tel-ef-on-oh)
I was just about to phone you when you knocked at the door. (informal)	Estaba a punto de telefonearte cuando tocaste a la puerta. (es-tah-bah a poon-toe dey tel-ef-own-ay-ar-tay kwan-doh toe-kas-tey a la pwer-ta)
I was just about to order a taxi when it started (literally "commenced") to rain.	Estaba a punto de reservar un taxi cuando comenzó a llover. (es-tah-bah a poon-toe dey re-surv-ar oon taxi kwan-doh emp-ess-oh / emp-eth-oh a yove-air)

That's it. Go and take your well-deserved break!

Forget what you were taught at school!

Many of us were told at school that we did not have an aptitude for languages, that we didn't have a "knack" or a "gift" for them.

Well, if this applies to you, then please let me assure you that this is all absolute nonsense! If you are able to read these words in front of you, then this demonstrates that you've been able to learn English and, if you can learn one language, then your brain is just as capable of learning another – it simply needs to be approached in the right way!

In fact, if you've got as far as Chapter 5, it should already be obvious to you that you are quite capable of learning a foreign language when it's taught in the right way. The secret of success for you will be choosing the right materials once you're finished with this book (more on that later).

CHAPTER 6 (1)

I'm sorry, I was busy preparing
the dinner when you arrived,
so I was a bit distracted. (part 1)

> I'm sorry, I was busy preparing the dinner when you arrived, so I was a bit distracted.

Isn't it annoying when people turn up just as you're busy doing something? And how much worse it is that you then need to apologise to them for ignoring them when they do.

Still, that is life, so you'd better get ready to deal with it in Spanish!

So, remind me, how would you say "I was about to..." (literally "I was at point of") in Spanish?

Estaba a punto de...
(es-tah-bah a poon-toe dey)

And how would you say "I was about to book a taxi"?

Estaba a punto de reservar un taxi.
(es-tah-bah a poon-toe dey re-surv-ar oon taxi)

How about "I was about to pay the bill"?

Estaba a punto de pagar la cuenta.
(es-tah-bah a poon-toe dey pag-ar la kwen-ta)

And "I was about to prepare the dinner"?

Estaba a punto de preparar la cena.
(es-tah-bah a poon-toe dey pre-par-ar la say-ner / thay-ner)

Now you may well be thinking, "what on earth is this?"

Well, the names Mario and María tell us something very interesting about Spanish.

They show us that male or masculine things in the Spanish language tend to end with an "o" – like the name "Mario" – but that female or feminine things tend to end with an "a" – like the name "María".

In Spanish, however, this affects more than just people's names. It also affects, for instance, the words that we use to describe those people.

For example, if you want to say "Mario is romantic" in Spanish, you will say:

Mario *es* romántico.
(ma-ree-oh *es* roe-man-tick-oh)

You will notice that there is an "o" on the end of both "Mario" and the Spanish word for "romantic" (romántico).

With this in mind, can you guess how you would say "María is romantic" in Spanish?

María *es* romántica.
(ma-ree-a *es* roe-man-tick-a)

So, here we can see that the word for "romantic" changes depending on whether it is describing someone male (masculine) or female (feminine). For masculine, we put an "o" on the end of the describing word and for feminine we put an "a". This is the Mario-María Rule in action.

So, now that you're familiar with this rule, how would you say "Mario is illogical"?

Mario es ilógico.
(ma-ree-oh es ee-lo-hee-koh)

And how would you say "María is illogical"?

María es ilógica.
(ma-ree-a es ee-lo-hee-ka)

And again, how would you say "I was" in Spanish?

Estaba
(es-tah-bah)

The word for describing someone male as "busy" or "occupied" in Spanish is:

ocupado
(*occ-oopa-doh*)

So, how would a man say "I was busy"?

Estaba ocupado.
(*estaba occ-oopa-doh*)

And so how do you think a woman would say "I was busy"?

Estaba ocupada.
(*estaba occ-oopa-da*)

So here we can see again here how, just as happened with words like "illogical" or "romantic", the word for "busy" changes depending on whether it is describing someone male (masculine) or female (feminine). It doesn't matter whether we're describing someone else or ourselves, we need to put an "o" on the Spanish word for someone masculine and an "a" for someone feminine.

Let's try another one!

The word for describing someone male as "distracted" in Spanish is:

distraído
(dis-tray-doh)

So, how would a man say "I was distracted"?

Estaba distraído.
(es-tah-bah dis-tray-doh)

And so how would a woman say the same thing?

Estaba distraída.
(es-tah-bah dis-tray-da)

Good. If you can work those out then that means you understand the basics of the Mario-María Rule. You are now ready to get on with building that sentence we started out with at the beginning of the chapter.

CHAPTER 6 (2)

I'm sorry, I was busy preparing
the dinner when you arrived,
so I was a bit distracted. (part 2)

> I'm sorry, I was busy preparing the dinner when you arrived, so I was a bit distracted.

So, again, what was "I was about to…" (literally "I was at point of") in Spanish?

Estaba a punto de…
(es-tah-bah a poon-toe dey)

And how would you say "I was about to prepare the dinner"?

Estaba a punto de preparar la cena.
(es-tah-bah a poon-toe dey pre-par-ar la say-ner / thay-ner)

Now again, do you remember how a man would say "I was busy" (literally "I was occupied")?

Estaba ocupado.
(es-tah-ba ok-oo-pah-doh)

And how would a woman say "I was busy"?

Estaba ocupada.
(es-tah-bah ok-oo-pah-da)

"Preparing" in Spanish is:

preparando
(pre-par-and-oh)

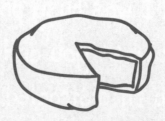

So, whereas we add an "ing" onto the ends of words in English, in Spanish they add "ando". (And it's always "ando" whether it's a man or a woman doing the preparing. So don't worry, the Spanish "ing" (ando) is not affected by the Mario-María rule!)

So, given that "preparing" is "preparando" how would you say "...preparing the dinner"?

peparando la cena
(pre-par-and-oh la say-ner / thay-ner)

And again, what was "I was busy"?

Estaba ocupado / ocupada.[13]
(es-tah-ba ok-oo-pah-doh / ok-oo-pah-da)

And so how would you say "I was busy preparing the dinner"

Estaba ocupado / ocupada peparando la cena.
(es-tah-ba ok-oo-pah-doh / ok-oo-pah-da pre-par-and-oh la say-ner / thay-ner)

---

13   So, depending on whether you're a man or woman, you'll choose either the masculine or feminine version of the word you're using to describe yourself.

"Reserving" or "booking" in Spanish is:

reservando
(re-surv-and-oh)

So how would you say "I was busy booking a taxi"?

Estaba ocupado / ocupada reservando un taxi.
(es-tah-ba ok-oo-pah-doh / ok-oo-pah-da re-surv-and-oh oon taxi)

And what is "the dinner" in Spanish?

la cena
(la say-ner / thay-ner)

"Having dinner" or, more literally, "dining" in Spanish is:

cenando
(say-nan-doh / thay-nan-doh)

So, how would you say "I was busy having dinner" (literally "I was occupied dining")?

Estaba ocupado / ocupada cenando.
(es-tah-ba ok-oo-pah-doh / ok-oo-pah-da say-nan-doh / thay-nan-doh)

What is the word for "when" in Spanish?

cuando
(kwan-doh)

"You arrived" (informal) in Spanish is:

Llegaste
(ye-gah-stay)

So, how would you say "...when you arrived" (informal)?

...*cuando llegaste*
(kwan-doh ye-gah-stay)

And again, how would you say "I was busy..."?

Estaba ocupado / ocupada...
(es-tah-ba ok-oo-pah-doh / ok-oo-pah-da)

And what about "I was busy preparing the dinner"?

Estaba ocupado / ocupada peparando la cena.
(es-tah-ba ok-oo-pah-doh / ok-oo-pah-da pre-par-and-oh la say-ner /
thay-ner)

And "I was busy having dinner"?

Estaba ocupado / ocupada cenando.
(es-tah-ba ok-oo-pah-doh / ok-oo-pah-da say-nan-doh / thay-nan-doh)

How about "I was busy having dinner when you arrived" (informal)?

Estaba ocupado / ocupada cenando cuando llegaste.
(es-tah-ba ok-oo-pah-doh / ok-oo-pah-da say-nan-doh / thay-nan-doh
kwan-doh ye-gah-stay)

And "I was busy preparing the dinner when you arrived" (informal)?

Estaba ocupado / ocupada peparando la cena cuando llegaste.
(es-tah-ba ok-oo-pah-doh / ok-oo-pah-da pre-par-and-oh la say-ner /
thay-ner kwan-doh ye-gah-stay)

To say "sorry" in Spanish you will say "I feel it" or "I sense it", which is:

lo siento
(lo see-en-toe)

The "lo" is the part that means "it" and the "siento" is the part that means "I feel"
or "I sense". So, "I'm sorry" in Spanish is, in absolutely literal terms, "it I feel" or
"it I sense".

So, how would you say "I'm sorry, I was busy preparing the dinner when you arrived" (informal)?

Lo siento, estaba ocupado / ocupada preparando la cena cuando llegaste.
(lo see-en-toe, es-tah-ba ok-oo-pah-doh / ok-oo-pah-da pre-par-and-oh la say-ner / thay-ner kwan-doh ye-gah-stay)

And how would you say "I'm sorry, I was busy having dinner when you arrived" (informal)?

Lo siento, estaba ocupado / ocupada cenando cuando llegaste.
(lo see-en-toe, es-tah-ba ok-oo-pah-doh / ok-oo-pah-da say-nan-doh / thay-nan-doh kwan-doh ye-gah-stay)

What was the masculine word for "distracted" in Spanish?

distraído
(dis-tray-doh)

And what was the feminine word for "distracted"?

distraída
(dis-tray-da)

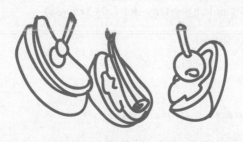

So, how would you say "I was distracted"?

Estaba distraído / distraída.
(estaba dis-tray-doh / dis-tray-da)

Now again, what was the word for "so" in Spanish?

por lo que
(poor-low-kay)

So, how would you say "...so I was distracted"?

... por lo que estaba distraído / distraída
(poor-low-kee es-tah-bah dis-tray-doh / dis-tray-da)

"A bit" or "a little" in Spanish is:

un poco
(oon pock-oh)

So, how would you say "...so I was a bit distracted"?

...por lo que estaba un poco distraído / distraída
(poor-low-kee es-tah-bah oon pock-oh dis-tray-doh / dis-tray-da)

And again, what is "I'm sorry"?

Lo siento.
(lo see-en-toe)

And what is "I was busy..."?

Estaba ocupado / ocupada...
(es-tah-ba ok-oo-pah-doh / ok-oo-pah-da)

So how would you say "I'm sorry, I was busy having dinner when you arrived" (informal)

Lo siento, estaba ocupado / ocupada cenando cuando llegaste.
(lo see-en-toe, es-tah-ba ok-oo-pah-doh / ok-oo-pah-da say-nan-doh / thay-nan-doh kwan-doh ye-gah-stay)

What about "I'm sorry, I was busy preparing the dinner when you arrived" (informal)?

Lo siento, estaba ocupado / ocupada peparando la cena cuando llegaste.
(lo see-en-toe, es-tah-ba ok-oo-pah-doh / ok-oo-pah-da pre-par-and-oh la say-ner / thay-ner kwan-doh ye-gah-stay)

Finally, let's imagine you had been preparing a dinner for some special guests when your friend came over to see you, and say "I'm sorry, I was busy preparing the dinner when you arrived, so I was a bit distracted" (informal)?

Lo siento, estaba ocupado / ocupada peparando la cena cuando llegaste, por lo que estaba un poco distraído / distraída.
(lo see on too, es tah ba ok oo pah doh / ok-oo-pah-da pre-par-and-oh la say-ner / thay-ner kwan-doh ye-gah-stay, poor-low-kee es-tah-bah oon pock-oh dis-tray-doh / dis-tray-da)

Well done with that! Again, take your time practising that last sentence until you feel confident constructing it. There's never a need to rush on to the next section until you feel you have properly finished with the previous one.

Sixth chapter, six new building blocks:

ordenando la casa
(or-den-an-doh
las ca-sa)
tidying the house

pintando
(peen-tan-doh)
painting

cuando llegó tu carta
(kwan-doh yeg-oh
too car-ta)
**when your letter
arrived** *1

cuando me llamaste
(kwan-doh may
yah-mah-stay)
when you called me
(informal)

hablando por teléfono
(ah-blan-doh por
te-ley-foh-noh)
**speaking on the
telephone**

cuando llegó mi madre
(kwan-doh yeg-oh
mee mar-dray)
**when my mother
arrived** *2

*1 literally "when arrived your letter"

*2 literally "when arrived my mother"

Now build me some sentences, please!

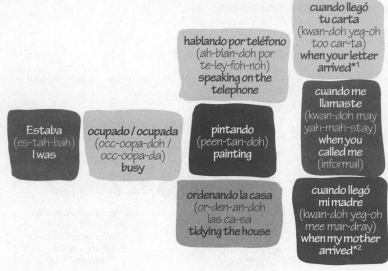

cuando llegó tu carta
(kwan-doh yeg-oh too car-ta)
when your letter arrived*¹

hablando por teléfono
(ah-blan-doh por te-ley-foh-noh)
speaking on the telephone

cuando me llamaste
(kwan-doh may yah-mah-stay)
when you called me
(informal)

Estaba
(es-tah-bah)
I was

ocupado / ocupada
(occ-oopa-doh / occ-oopa-da)
busy

pintando
(peen-tan-doh)
painting

ordenando la casa
(or-den-an-doh las ca-sa)
tidying the house

cuando llegó mi madre
(kwan-doh yeg-oh mee mar-dray)
when my mother arrived*²

*¹ literally "when arrived your letter"

*² literally "when arrived my mother"

Checklist 6

Checklist number 6, take your time and enjoy it (if you can)!

el fin de semana (el fin dey sem-arn-er)	the weekend
romántico (roe-man-tick-oh)	romantic
típico (tip-ick-oh)	typical
político (po-li-tick-oh)	political
lógico (lo-hee-koh)	logical
histórico (ee-sto-rick-oh)	historical
crítico (kri-tick-oh)	critical
clásico (clas-ick-oh)	classical
eléctrico (el-ek-trick-oh)	electrical
idéntico (ee-dent-ick-oh)	identical
biológico (bee-oh-lo-hee-koh)	biological
entusiasmado (en-tooz-ee-as-mard-oh)	enthusiastic
Visité (visit-ay)	I visited
Barcelona (bar-sair-loan-er / bar-thair-loan-er)	Barcelona
Madrid (ma-drid)	Madrid
Visité Madrid. (visit-ay ma-drid)	I visited Madrid.
Pasé (pass-ay)	I spent
Pasó (pass-o)	You spent
Pasamos (pass-arm-oss)	We spent
septiembre (sep-tee-em-brey)	September
la Navidad (la na-vee-dad)	Christmas (literally "the Christmas")
en Barcelona (en bar-sair-loan-er / bar-thair-loan-er)	in Barcelona

en España (en es-pan-ya)	in Spain
en México (en me-hee-koe)	in Mexico
Pasamos la Navidad en México. (pass-arm-oss la na-vee-dad en me-hee-koe)	We spent Christmas in Mexico.
Pasó septiembre en España. (pass-o sep-tee-em-brey en es-pan-ya)	You spent September in Spain.
y (ee)	and
fue (fway)	it was
fue romántico (fway roe-man-tick-oh)	it was romantic
adorable (ad-or-arb-lay)	lovely / adorable
fue adorable (fway ad-or-arb-lay)	it was lovely / it was adorable
Pasé el fin de semana en Barcelona… y fue adorable. (pass-ay el fin dey sem-arn-er en bar-sair-loan-er / bar-thair-loan-er ee fway ad-or-arb-lay)	I spent the weekend in Barcelona… and it was lovely.
invitación (in-vit-ass-ee-on)	invitation
Invité (in-vit-ay)	I invited
preparación (pray-par-ass-ee-on)	preparation
Preparé (pre-par-ay)	I prepared
reservación (re-surv-ass-ee-on / re-surv-ath-ee-on)	reservation (preferred in Latin American)
reserva (re-surv-a)	reservation (preferred in Spain)
Reservé (re-surv-ay)	I reserved / booked
cooperación (cope-air-ass-ee-on / cope-air-ath-ee-on)	cooperation
Cooperé (cope-air-ay)	I cooperated
imaginación (im-a-hin-ass-ee-on / im-a-hin-ath-ee-on)	imagination
Imaginé (im-a-hin-ay)	I imagined
manipulación (man-ip-ool-ass-ee-on / man-ip-ool-ath-ee-on)	manipulation

Manipulé (man-ip-ool-ay)	I manipulated
continuación (con-tin-oo-ass-ee-on / con-tin-oo-ath-ee-on)	continuation
Continué (con-tin-oo-ay)	I continued
participación (par-tis-ip-ass-ee-on / par-tith-ip-ath-ee-on)	participation
Participé (par-tis-ip-ay / par-tith-ip-ay)	I participated
exageración (ex-a-hair-ass-ee-on / ex-a-hair-ath-ee-on)	exaggeration
Exageré (ex-a-hair ay)	I exaggerated
admiración (ad-mi-rass-ee-on / ad-mi-rath-ee-on)	admiration
Admiré (ad-mi-ray)	I admired
irritación (ee-ri-tass-ee-on / ee-ri-tath-ee-on)	irritation
Irrité (ee-ri-tay)	I irritated
conversación (con-vair-sass-ee-on / con-vair-sath-ee-on)	conversation
Conversé (con-vair-say)	I conversed
Ordené (or-den-ay)	I ordered (preferred in Latin American)
Pedí (pe-dee)	I ordered (literally "I asked for") – (preferred in Spain)
Paqué (pag-ay)	I paid
Hice (ee-say / ee-thay)	I did
la cuenta (la kwen-ta)	the bill
la cena (la say-ner / thay-ner)	the dinner
sopa (soap-er)	soup
una mesa (oon-er may-ser)	a table
una habitación (oon-er ab-it-ass-ee-on / ab-it-ath-ee-on)	a room
un taxi (oon taxi)	a taxi
Preparé la cena. (pre-par-ay la say-ner / thay-ner)	I prepared the dinner.

Ordené sopa para la cena. (or-den-ay soap-er pa-ra la say-ner / thay-ner)	I ordered soup for dinner. (preferred in Latin American)
Pedí sopa para la cena. (pe-dee soap-er pa-ra la say-ner / thay-ner)	I ordered soup for dinner. (preferred in Spain)
Reservé una mesa para usted. (re-surv-ay oon-er may-ser pa-ra oo-stedd)	I booked a table for you.
Ella reservó (ay-a re-surv-o)	She booked / reserved
Ella reservó una mesa para esta noche. (ay-a re-surv-ay oon-er may-ser pa-ra es-ta noch-ay)	She booked / reserved a table for this evening.
Él reservó (el re-surv-o)	He booked / reserved
Él reservó una habitación para dos personas. (el re-surv-o oon-er ab-it-ass-ee-on / ab-it-ath-ee-on pa-ra doss pair-so-nass)	He booked / reserved a room for two people.
¿Qué? (kay)	What?
¿Qué preparó? (kay pre-par-o)	What did you prepare?
¿Qué preparó usted? (kay pre-par-o oo-sted)	What did you prepare?
¿Qué hizo usted? (kay ee-soe / ee-thoe oo-sted)	What did you do?
Reservé una mesa, ordené la cena y luego pagué la cuenta. ¿Qué hizo usted? (re-surv-ay oon-er may-ser, or-den-ay la say-ner / thay-ner ee loo-way-go pag-ay la kwen-ta. kay ee-soe / ee-thoe oo-sted)	I booked a table, ordered dinner and then paid the bill. What did you do?
Tengo la intención de… (ten-go la in-ten-see-on / in-ten-thee-on dey)	I'm planning to… (literally "I have the intention of…")
Tengo la intención de volver a España en mayo. (ten-go la in-ten-see-on / in-ten-thee-on dey vol-vair a es-pan-ya en my-oh)	I'm planning to go back to Spain in May.
Tengo miedo de… (ten-go mee-ed-oh dey)	I'm scared of… (literally "I have fear of…")

Tengo miedo de volver a España en septiembre. (ten-go mee-ed-oh dey vol-vair a es-pan-ya en sep-tee-em-brey)	I'm scared of going back to Spain in September.
¿De verdad? (dey vair-dad)	Really?
por lo que (poor-low-kay)	so
pero (pair-o)	but
Tengo ganas de... (ten-go ga-nas dey)	I feel like... / I fancy... (literally "I have desire of...")
Sí, tengo ganas de volver a Barcelona, pero tengo miedo de volar, por lo que tengo la intención de tomar el Eurostar. (see ten-go ga-nas dey vol-vair a bar-sair-loan-er / bar-thair-loan-er pair o ten-go mee-ed-oh dey vol-ar, poor-low-kay ten-go la in-ten-see-on / in-ten-thee-on dey to-mar el e-oo-roe-star)	Yes, I feel like going back to Barcelona but I'm scared of flying, so I'm planning to take the Eurostar.
Tengo ganas de comprar algo esta mañana. (ten-go ga-nas dey com-prar al-go es-ta man-yarn-a)	I feel like / fancy buying something this morning.
Tengo ganas de leer algo esta tarde. (ten-go ga-nas dey lay-air al-go es-ta tar dey)	I feel like / fancy reading something this afternoon.
Tiene (tee-en-ey)	You have (formal)
Tiene ganas de comer algo esta noche. (tee-en-ey ga-nas dey kom-air al-go es-ta noch-ay)	You feel like eating something this evening. (formal)
Necesito (ness-e-seet-oh / neth-e-seet-oh)	I need
Necesito hablar español. (ness-e-seet-oh / neth-e-seet-oh a-blar es-pa-nyol)	I need to speak Spanish.
Necesito un taxi. (ness-e-seet-oh / neth-e-seet oh oon taxi)	I need a taxi.

Necesito una habitación. (ness-e-seet-oh / neth-e-seet-oh oon-er ab-it-ass-ee-on / ab-it-ath-ee-on)	I need a room.
Necesito ayuda. (ness-e-seet-oh / neth-e-seet-oh a-yoo-der)	I need help.
¡Necesitas ayuda, camarada! (ness-e-seet-ass / neth-e-seet-ass a-yoo-der ca-ma-ra-da)	You need help, mate!
Odio (oh-dee-oh)	I hate
¡Odio volar! (oh-dee-oh vol-ar)	I hate flying!
Odio vivir con mis suegros. (odio viv-eer kon miss soo-egg-ros)	I hate living with my in-laws.
Odias comer con mis padres. (oh-dee-ass sey-nan-doh kon miss pard-res)	You hate having dinner with my parents. (informal)
Odia trabajar aquí. (oh-dee-a trab-a-har a-key)	You hate working here. (formal)
Estaba (es-tah-bah)	I was
solitario (so-lit-ar-ee-oh)	solitary
contrario (kon-trar-ee-oh)	contrary
ordinario (or-din-ar-ee-oh)	ordinary
Estaba a punto de... (es-tah-bah a poon-toe dey)	I was about to... / I was just about to... (literally "I was at point of...")
Estaba a punto de preparar la cena. (es-tah-bah a poon-toe dey pre-par-ar la say-ner / thay-ner)	I was about to prepare the dinner / I was just about to prepare the dinner.
Estaba a punto de pagar la cuenta. (es-tah-bah a poon-toe dey pag-ar la kwen-ta)	I was about to pay the bill.
Estaba a punto de reservar una mesa. (es-tah-bah a poon-toe dey re-surv-ar oon-er may-ser)	I was just about to book a table.
Me llamaste. (may yah-mah-stay)	You called me / You did call me / You have called me. (informal)

cuando (kwan-doh)	when
Estaba a punto de reservar un taxi cuando me llamaste. (es-tah-bah a poon-toe dey re-surv-ar oon taxi kwan-doh may yah-mah-stay.)	I was just about to book a taxi when you called me.
Estaba a punto de salir cuando sonó el teléfono. (es-tah-bah a poon-toe dey sal-ear kwan-doh sonn-oh el tel-ef-on-oh)	I was about to leave when the telephone rang.
Estaba a punto de telefonearte cuando tocaste a la puerta. (es-tah-bah a poon-toe dey tel-ef-own-ay-ar-tay kwan-doh toe-kas-tey a la pwer-ta)	I was just about to phone you when you knocked at the door. (informal)
Estaba a punto de reservar un taxi cuando comenzó a llover. (es-tah-bah a poon-toe dey re-surv-ar oon taxi kwan-doh emp-ess-oh / emp-eth-oh a yove-air)	I was just about to order a taxi when it started (literally "commenced") to rain.
Llegaste. (ye-gah-stay)	You have arrived / You arrived / You did arrive. (informal)
Lo siento. (lo see-en-toe)	I'm sorry.
un poco (oon pock-oh)	a little / a bit
Estaba un poco distraído / distraída. (es-tah-bah oon pock-oh dis-tray-doh / dis-tray-da)	I was a little preoccupied / distracted.
Estaba ocupado / ocupada… (es-tah-bah occ-oopa-doh / occ-oopa-da)	I was busy…
Lo siento, estaba ocupado / ocupada cenando cuando llegaste. (lo see-en-toe, es-tah-bah occ-oopa-doh / occ-oopa-da sey-nan-doh kwan-doh ye-gah-stay)	I'm sorry, I was busy having dinner when you arrived. (informal)

Lo siento, estaba ocupado / ocupada preparando la cena cuando llegaste, por lo que estaba un poco distraído / distraída. (lo see-en-toe, es-tah-bah occ-oopa-doh / occ-oopa-da pre-par-and-oh la say-ner / thay-ner kwan-doh ye-gah-stay poor-low-kee es-tah-bah oon pock-oh dis-tray-doh / dis-tray-da)	I'm sorry, I was busy preparing the dinner when you arrived, so I was a bit distracted. (informal)
Estaba ocupado / ocupada ordenando la casa cuando llegó mi madre. (es-tah-bah occ-oopa-doh / occ-oopa-da or-de-nan-doh la ca-sa kwan-doh yeg-oh mee mar-dray)	I was busy tidying the house when my mother arrived.
Estaba ocupado / ocupada pintando cuando me llamaste. (es-tah-bah occ-oopa-doh / occ-oopa-da peen-tan-doh kwan-doh may yah-mah-stay)	I was busy painting when you called me.
Estaba ocupado / ocupada hablando por teléfono cuando llegó tu carta. (es-tah-bah occ-oopa-doh / occ-oopa-da ah-blan-doh por te-ley-foh-noh kwan-doh yeg-oh too car-ta)	I was busy speaking on the telephone when your letter arrived.

Now enjoy yourself doing it the other way round.

Twice the fun for half the effort... erm... kind of.

the weekend	**el fin de semana** (el fin dey sem-arn-er)
romantic	**romántico** (roe-man-tick-oh)
typical	**típico** (tip-ick-oh)
political	**político** (po-li-tick-oh)
logical	**lógico** (lo hee koh)
historical	**histórico** (ee-sto-rick-oh)
critical	**crítico** (kri-tick-oh)
classical	**clásico** (clas-ick-oh)
electrical	**eléctrico** (el-ek-trick-oh)
identical	**idéntico** (ee-dent-ick-oh)
biological	**biológico** (bee-oh-lo-hee-koh)
enthusiastic	**entusiasmado** (en-tooz-ee-as-mard-oh)
I visited	**Visité** (visit-ay)
Barcelona	**Barcelona** (bar-sair-loan-er / bar-thair-loan-er)
Madrid	**Madrid** (ma-drid)
I visited Madrid.	**Visité Madrid.** (visit-ay ma-drid)
I spent	**Pasé** (pass-ay)
You spent	**Pasó** (pass-o)
We spent	**Pasamos** (pass-arm-oss)
September	**septiembre** (sep-tee-em-brey)
Christmas (literally "the Christmas")	**la Navidad** (la na-vee-dad)
in Barcelona	**en Barcelona** (en bar-sair-loan-er / bar-thair-loan-er)
in Spain	**en España** (en es-pan-ya)
in Mexico	**en México** (en me-hee-koe)

We spent Christmas in Mexico.	Pasamos la Navidad en México. (pass-arm-oss la na-vee-dad en me-hee-koe)
You spent September in Spain.	Pasó septiembre en España. (pass-o sep-tee-em-brey en es-pan-ya)
and	y (ee)
it was	fue (fway)
it was romantic	fue romántico (fway roe-man-tick-oh)
lovely / adorable	adorable (ad-or-arb-lay)
it was lovely / it was adorable	fue adorable (fway ad-or-arb-lay)
I spent the weekend in Barcelona... and it was lovely.	Pasé el fin de semana en Barcelona... y fue adorable. (pass-ay el fin dey sem-arn-er en bar-sair-loan-er / bar-thair-loan-er ee fway ad-or-arb-lay)
invitation	invitación (in-vit-ass-ee-on)
I invited	Invité (in-vit-ay)
preparation	preparación (pray-par-ass-ee-on)
I prepared	Preparé (pre-par-ay)
reservation (preferred in Latin American)	reservación (re-surv-ass-ee-on / re-surv-ath-ee-on)
reservation (preferred in Spain)	reserva (re-surv-a)
I reserved / booked	Reservé (re-surv-ay)
cooperation	cooperación (cope-air-ass-ee-on / cope-air-ath-ee-on)
I cooperated	Cooperé (cope-air-ay)
imagination	imaginación (im-a-hin-ass-ee-on / im-a-hin-ath-ee-on)
I imagined	Imaginé (im-a-hin-ay)
manipulation	manipulación (man-ip-ool-ass-ee-on / man-ip-ool-ath-ee-on)
I manipulated	Manipulé (man-ip-ool-ay)
continuation	continuación (con-tin-oo-ass-ee-on / con-tin-oo-ath-ee-on)

I continued	Continué (con-tin-oo-ay)
participation	participación (par-tis-ip-ass-ee-on / par-tith-ip-ath-ee-on)
I participated	Participé (par-tis-ip-ay / par-tith-ip-ay)
exaggeration	exageración (ex-a-hair-ass-ee-on / ex-a-hair-ath-ee-on)
I exaggerated	Exageré (ex-a-hair-ay)
admiration	admiración (ad-mi-rass-ee-on / ad-mi-rath-ee-on)
I admired	Admiré (ad-mi-ray)
irritation	irritación (ee-ri-tass-ee-on / ee-ri-tath-ee-on)
I irritated	Irrité (ee-ri-tay)
conversation	conversación (con-vair-sass-ee-on / con-vair-sath-ee-on)
I conversed	Conversé (con-vair-say)
I ordered (preferred in Latin American)	Ordené (or-den-ay)
I ordered (literally "I asked for") – (preferred in Spain)	Pedí (pe-dee)
I paid	Pagué (pag-ay)
I did	Hice (ee-say / ee-thay)
the bill	la cuenta (la kwen-ta)
the dinner	la cena (la say-ner / thay-ner)
soup	sopa (soap-er)
a table	una mesa (oon-er may-ser)
a room	una habitación (oon-er ab-it-ass-ee-on / ab-it-ath-ee-on)
a taxi	un taxi (oon taxi)
I prepared the dinner.	Preparé la cena. (pre-par-ay la say-ner / thay-ner)
I ordered soup for dinner. (preferred in Latin American)	Ordené sopa para la cena. (or-den-ay soap-er pa-ra la say-ner / thay-ner)

I ordered soup for dinner. (preferred in Spain)	Pedí sopa para la cena. (pe-dee soap-er pa-ra la say-ner / thay-ner)
I booked a table for you.	Reservé una mesa para usted. (re-surv-ay oon-er may-ser pa-ra oo-stedd)
She booked / reserved	Ella reservó (ay-a re-surv-o)
She booked / reserved a table for this evening.	Ella reservó una mesa para esta noche. (ay-a re-surv-ay oon-er may-ser pa-ra es-ta noch-ay)
He booked / reserved	Él reservó (el re-surv-o)
He booked / reserved a room for two people.	Él reservó una habitación para dos personas. (el re-surv-o oon-er ab-it-ass-ee-on / ab-it-ath-ee-on pa-ra doss pair-so-nass)
What?	¿Qué? (kay)
What did you prepare?	¿Qué preparó? (kay pre-par-o)
What did you prepare?	¿Qué preparó usted? (kay pre-par-o oo-sted)
What did you do?	¿Qué hizo usted? (kay ee-soe / ee-thoe oo-sted)
I booked a table, ordered dinner and then paid the bill. What did you do?	Reservé una mesa, ordené la cena y luego pagué la cuenta. ¿Qué hizo usted? (re-surv-ay oon-er may-ser, or-den-ay la say-ner / thay-ner ee loo-way-go pag-ay la kwen-ta. kay ee-soe / ee-thoe oo-sted)
I'm planning to… (literally "I have the intention of…")	Tengo la intención de… (ten-go la in-ten-see-on / in-ten-thee-on dey)
I'm planning to go back to Spain in May.	Tengo la intención de volver a España en mayo. (ten-go la in-ten-see-on / in-ten-thee-on dey vol-vair a es-pan-ya en my-oh)
I'm scared of… (literally "I have fear of…")	Tengo miedo de… (ten-go mee-ed-oh dey)

I'm scared of going back to Spain in September.	**Tengo miedo de volver a España en septiembre.** (ten-go mee-ed-oh dey vol-vair a es-pan-ya en sep-tee-em-brey)
Really?	**¿De verdad?** (dey vair-dad)
so	**por lo que** (poor-low-kay)
but	**pero** (pair o)
I feel like… / I fancy… (literally "I have desire of…")	**Tengo ganas de…** (ten-go ga-nas dey)
Yes, I feel like going back to Barcelona but I'm scared of flying, so I'm planning to take the Eurostar.	**Sí, tengo ganas de volver a Barcelona, pero tengo miedo de volar, por lo que tengo la intención de tomar el Eurostar.** (see ten-go ga-nas dey vol-vair a bar-sair-loan-er / bar-thair-loan-er pair-o ten-go mee-ed-oh dey vol-ar, poor-low-kay ten-go la in-ten-see-on / in-ten-thee-on dey to-mar el e-oo-roe-star)
I feel like / fancy buying something this morning.	**Tengo ganas de comprar algo esta mañana.** (ten-go ga-nas dey com-prar al-go es-ta man-yarn-a)
I feel like / fancy reading something this afternoon.	**Tengo ganas de leer algo esta tarde.** (ten-go ga-nas dey lay-air al-go es-ta tar-dey)
You have (formal)	**Tiene** (tee-en-ey)
You feel like eating something this evening. (formal)	**Tiene ganas de comer algo esta noche.** (tee-en-ey ga-nas dey kom-air al-go es-ta noch-ay)
I need	**Necesito** (ness-e-seet-oh / neth-e-seet-oh)
I need to speak Spanish.	**Necesito hablar español.** (ness-e-seet-oh / neth-e-seet-oh a-blar es-pa-nyol)
I need a taxi.	**Necesito un taxi.** (ness-e-seet-oh / neth-e-seet-oh oon taxi)

I need a room.	Necesito una habitación. (ness-e-seet-oh / neth-e-seet-oh oon-er ab-it-ass-ee-on / ab-it-ath-ee-on)
I need help.	Necesito ayuda. (ness-e-seet-oh / neth-e-seet-oh a-yoo-der)
You need help, mate!	¡Necesitas ayuda, camarada! (ness-e-seet-ass / neth-e-seet-ass a-yoo-der ca-ma-ra-da)
I hate	Odio (oh-dee-oh)
I hate flying!	¡Odio volar! (oh-dee-oh vol-ar)
I hate living with my in-laws.	Odio vivir con mis suegros. (odio viv-eer kon miss soo-egg-ros)
You hate having dinner with my parents. (informal)	Odias comer con mis padres. (oh-dee-ass sey-nan-doh kon miss pard-res)
You hate working here. (formal)	Odia trabajar aquí. (oh-dee-a trab-a-har a-key)
I was	Estaba (es-tah-bah)
solitary	solitario (so-lit-ar-ee-oh)
contrary	contrario (kon-trar-ee-oh)
ordinary	ordinario (or-din-ar-ee-oh)
I was about to... / I was just about to... (literally "I was at point of...")	Estaba a punto de... (es-tah-bah a poon-toe dey)
I was about to prepare the dinner / I was just about to prepare the dinner.	Estaba a punto de preparar la cena. (es-tah-bah a poon-toe dey pre-par-ar la say-ner / thay-ner)
I was about to pay the bill.	Estaba a punto de pagar la cuenta. (es-tah-bah a poon-toe dey pag-ar la kwen-ta)
I was just about to book a table.	Estaba a punto de reservar una mesa. (es-tah-bah a poon-toe dey re-surv-ar oon-er may-ser)
You called me / You did call me / You have called me. (informal)	Me llamaste. (may yah-mah-stay)

when	cuando (kwan-doh)
I was just about to book a taxi when you called me.	Estaba a punto de reservar un taxi cuando me llamaste. (es-tah-bah a poon-toe dey re-surv-ar oon taxi kwan-doh may yah-mah-stay.)
I was about to leave when the telephone rang.	Estaba a punto de salir cuando sonó el teléfono. (es-tah-bah a poon-toe dey sal-ear kwan-doh sonn-oh el tel-ef-on-oh)
I was just about to phone you when you knocked at the door. (informal)	Estaba a punto de telefonearte cuando tocaste a la puerta. (es-tah-bah a poon-toe dey tel-ef-own-ay-ar-tay kwan-doh toe-kas-tey a la pwer-ta)
I was just about to order a taxi when it started (literally "commenced") to rain.	Estaba a punto de reservar un taxi cuando comenzó a llover. (es-tah-bah a poon-toe dey re-surv-ar oon taxi kwan-doh emp-ess-oh / emp-eth-oh a yove-air)
You have arrived / You arrived / You did arrive. (informal)	Llegaste. (ye-gah-stay)
I'm sorry.	Lo siento. (lo see-en-toe)
a little / a bit	un poco (oon pock-oh)
I was a little preoccupied / distracted.	Estaba un poco distraído / distraída. (es-tah-bah oon pock-oh dis-tray-doh / dis-tray-da)
I was busy...	Estaba ocupado / ocupada... (es-tah-bah occ-oopa-doh / occ-oopa-da)
I'm sorry, I was busy having dinner when you arrived. (informal)	Lo siento, estaba ocupado / ocupada cenando cuando llegaste. (lo see-en-toe, es-tah-bah occ-oopa-doh / occ-oopa-da sey-nan-doh kwan-doh ye-gah-stay)

I'm sorry, I was busy preparing the dinner when you arrived, so I was a bit distracted. (informal)	Lo siento, estaba ocupado / ocupada preparando la cena cuando llegaste, por lo que estaba un poco distraído / distraída. (lo see-en-toe, es-tah-bah occ-oopa-doh / occ-oopa-da pre-par-and-oh la say-ner / thay-ner kwan-doh ye-gah-stay poor-low-kee es-tah-bah oon pock-oh dis-tray-doh / dis-tray-da)
I was busy tidying the house when my mother arrived.	Estaba ocupado / ocupada ordenando la casa cuando llegó mi madre. (es-tah-bah occ-oopa-doh / occ-oopa-da or-de-nan-doh la ca-sa kwan-doh yeg-oh mee mar-dray)
I was busy painting when you called me.	Estaba ocupado / ocupada pintando cuando me llamaste. (es-tah-bah occ-oopa-doh / occ-oopa-da peen-tan-doh kwan-doh may yah-mah-stay)
I was busy speaking on the telephone when your letter arrived.	Estaba ocupado / ocupada hablando por teléfono cuando llegó tu carta. (es-tah-bah occ-oopa-doh / occ-oopa-da ah-blan-doh por te-ley-foh-noh kwan-doh yeg-oh too car-ta)

Wow, Chapter 6 all finished! With each chapter completed, the knowledge you have already gained becomes more secure and your horizons are gradually widened. Have a good break before the next one!

Between Chapters Tip!

Learn the most common words first

Did you know that the 100 most common words in a language make up roughly 50% of everything you say in any given day, week, month or year? Or that the 500 most common words make up roughly 90% of everything you say?

Since these extremely common words are so useful, I recommend that, in addition to stealing words wherever you can, you should also focus as much as possible on those words that are used most often, as these will form the backbone of everything you say.

Of course, you may be wondering, how do I know which words are most common? Well, one way to find this out is to look at word frequency lists that you can find on the internet – boring!

Another way, though, is to note down unfamiliar words whenever you see them. Don't bother looking them up right away though. Instead, put a tick next to them every subsequent time that you come across them.

Then, at the end of every month, take a look and see which words have the most ticks against them – these are the most common. Feel free now to look these up and write the translation next to all the ticks you've made.

Having finished writing down the translation, don't try to remember it though – instead, whenever you encounter those same words again, flick back to your notes and check the meaning.

Doing this each time will guarantee that your focus will always be on the most common words and that you will gradually begin to pick them up!

CHAPTER 7

I'm moving to Spain in July
because of you!
BECAUSE of me?
You mean *THANKS* to me!

> I'm moving to Spain in July because of you!
> BECAUSE of me? You mean THANKS to me!

You help someone change their life and this is the thanks you get!

Well, you may already know how to be ungrateful in English, so let me teach you how to be ungrateful in Spanish.

What is "September" in Spanish?

septiembre
(sep-tee-em-brey)

And what is "in September" in Spanish?

en septiembre
(en sep-tee-em-brey)

What is "August" in Spanish?

agosto
(a-gost-oh)

So how would you say "in August"?

en agosto
(en a-gost-oh)

What is "May" in Spanish?

mayo
(my-oh)

So what would "in May" be?

en mayo
(en my-oh)

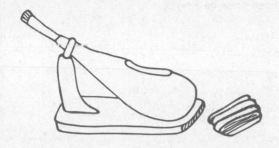

"July" in Spanish is:

julio
(hoo-lee-oh)

So, how would you say "in July"?

en julio
(en hoo-lee-oh)

And again, how would you say "I visited"?

Visité
(visit-ay)

And what about "I visited Barcelona"?

Visité Barcelona.
(visit-ay bar-sair-loan-er / bar-thair-loan-er)

So, how would you say "I visited Barcelona in July"?

Visité Barcelona en julio.
(visit-ay bar-sair-loan-er / bar-thair-loan-er en hoo-lee-oh)

What is "I'm planning to..."?

Tengo la intención de...
(ten-go la in-ten-see-on / in-ten-thee-on dey)

"Visit" or "to visit" in Spanish is:

visitar
(visit-ar)

So, how would you say "I'm planning to visit..."?

Tengo la intención de visitar...
(ten-go la in-ten-see-on / in-ten-thee-on dey visit-ar)

And how would you say "I'm planning to visit Barcelona in July"?

Tengo la intención de visitar Barcelona en julio.
(ten-go la in-ten-see-on / in-ten-thee-on dey visit-ar bar-sair-loan-er /
bar-thair-loan-er en hoo-lee-oh)

What is "to go back" in Spanish?

volver
(vol-vair)

So how would you say "I'm planning to go back"?

Tengo la intención de volver.
(ten-go la in-ten-see-on / in-ten-thee-on dey vol-vair)

And what is "to Spain"?

a España
(a es-pan-ya)

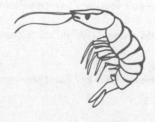

So, how would you say "I'm planning to go back to Spain in July"?

Tengo la intención de volver a España en julio.
(ten-go la in-ten-see-on / in-ten-thee-on dey vol-vair a es-pan-ya en hoo-lee-oh)

"I'm going" in Spanish is:

Voy
(voy)

And how would you say "to Spain"?

a España
(a es-pan-ya)

And so how would you say "I'm going to Spain"?

Voy a España.
(voy a es-pan-ya)

How about "I'm going to Spain in July"?

Voy a España en julio.
(voy a es-pan-ya en hoo-lee-oh)

What about "I'm going to Spain in September"?

Voy a España en septiembre.
(voy a es-pan-ya en sep-tee-em-brey)

And how would you say "to Barcelona"?

a Barcelona
(a bar-sair-loan-er / bar-thair-loan-er)

So, how would you say "I'm going to Barcelona in September"?

Voy a Barcelona en septiembre.
(voy a bar-sair-loan-er / bar-thair-loan-er en sep-tee-em-brey)

What is "for you" in Spanish?

para usted
(pa-ra oo-stedd)

So what is the word for "you" in Spanish?

usted
(oo-sted)

Remember that "usted" is the *formal* word for "you" in Spanish.

"Because of..." in Spanish is:

por...
(por)

So how would you say "because of you" (formal)?

por usted
(por oo-sted)

So, how would you say "I'm going to Barcelona in September because of you!" (formal)?

¡Voy a Barcelona en septiembre por usted!
(voy a bar-sair-loan-er / bar-thair-loan-er en sep-tee-em-brey a bar-sair-loan-er / bar-thair-loan-er por oo-sted)

Now try "I'm going to Barcelona in July because of you!" (formal).

¡Voy a Barcelona en julio por usted!
(voy a bar-sair-loan-er / bar-thair-loan-er en hoo-lee-oh por oo-sted)

What is "to Spain"?

a España
(a es-pan-ya)

So, how would you say "I'm going to Spain in July because of you!" (formal)?

¡Voy a España en julio por usted!
(voy a es-pan-ya en hoo-lee-oh por oo-sted)

"Because of you" (informal) in Spanish is:

por ti
(por tee)

So, how would you say "I'm going to Spain in July because of you!" (informal)?

¡Voy a España en julio por ti!
(voy a es-pan-ya en hoo-lee-oh por tee)

How about "I'm going to Barcelona in July because of you!" (informal)?

¡Voy a Barcelona en julio por ti!
(voy a bar-sair-loan-er / bar-thair-loan-er en hoo-lee-oh por tee)

"Because of me" in Spanish is:

por mí
(por mee)

So, turn this into a question by raising your voice at the end and ask "because of me?".

¿Por mí?
(por mee)

So, we have now learnt how to say "because of" in Spanish. It is a very useful phrase, which can be used both in a fairly neutral way or, if you want, in a very negative way to attribute blame: "I lost my money because of you!" or "I never got married because of you!" Heady stuff, yes!

"Because of" actually has a partner that has a similar meaning except that it is more positive and means "thanks to..." You will want to use this phrase for nice things, such as "Thanks to you, I found my money in the end" or "Thanks to you, I met and married a wonderful person!"

"Thanks to..." in Spanish is:

gracias a...
(gra-see-ass a)

So, how would you say "thanks to me!" (informal)?

¡Gracias a mí!
(gra-see-ass a mee)

And how about "thanks to you!" (informal)?

¡Gracias a ti!
(gra-see-ass a tee)

"Do you want?" (informal) in Spanish is:

¿Quieres?
(kee-air-es)

Literally, "quieres" means "you want" but if you raise your voice as you say it, it becomes a question, literally "you want?" – "¿quieres?"

So, how would you say "do you want to prepare the dinner?" (informal) – (literally "want you to prepare the dinner?")?

¿Quieres preparar la cena?
(kee-air-es pre-par-ar la say-ner / thay-ner)

What is "this evening" in Spanish?

esta noche
(*es-ta noch-ay*)

So, how would you say "do you want to prepare the dinner this evening?" (informal)
– (literally "want you to prepare the dinner this evening?")?

¿Quieres preparar la cena esta noche?
(*kee-air-es pre-par-ar la say-ner / thay-ner es-ta noch-ay*)

What is "to eat something"?

comer algo
(*sey-nan-doh al-go*)

So, how would you say "do you want to eat something?" (informal)?

¿Quieres comer algo?
(*kee-air-es sey-nan-doh al-go*)

How about "do you want to buy something?" (informal)?

¿Quieres comprar algo?
(*kee-air-es com-prar al-go*)

What is "to pay the bill"?

pagar la cuenta
(*pag-ar la kwen-ta*)

So, how would you say "do you want to pay the bill?" (informal)?

¿Quieres pagar la cuenta?
(kee-air-es pag-ar la kwen-ta)

How about "do you want to book a taxi?" (informal)?

¿Quieres reservar un taxi?
(kee-air-es ray-zur-var oon taxi)

"Do you want to go back to Spain in July?" (informal)?

¿Quieres volver a España en julio?
(kee-air-es vol-vair a es-pan-ya en hoo-lee-oh)

So "do you want?" (informal) as a question is:

¿Quieres?
(kee-air-es)

So, how would you say as a statment "you want to go back to Spain in July" (informal)?

Quieres volver a España en julio.
(kee-air-es vol-vair a es-pan-ya en hoo-lee-oh)

And how about "you want to go back to Barcelona in July" (informal)?

Quieres volver a Barcelona en julio.
(kee-air-es vol-vair a bar-sair-loan-er / bar-thair-loan-er en hoo-lee-oh)

And how would you say "you want to pay the bill" (informal)?

Quieres pagar la cuenta.
(kee-air-es pag-ar la kwen-ta)

"To say" in Spanish is:

decir
(de-seer / de-theer)

So, how would you say "you want to say" (informal)?

Quieres decir
(kee-air-es de-seer / de-theer)

Now, "you want to say" is actually the way that Spanish speakers say "you mean". So, if, for example, a Spanish person wants to say "what do you mean?", then they will ask "what do you want to say?"

So, to begin with, how would you say "you mean" in Spanish (informal) – (literally "you want to say")?

Quieres decir
(kee-air-es de-seer / de-theer)

And again what is "thanks to..."?

Gracias a...
(gra-see-ass a)

And "thanks to me"?

Gracias a mí.
(gra-see-ass a mee)

And once more, how would you say "you mean" (informal) – (literally "you want to say")?

Quieres decir
(kee-air-es de-seer / de-theer)

So how would you say "you mean thanks to me!" (informal)?

¡Quieres decir *gracias* a mí!
(kee-air-es de-seer / de-theer gra-see-ass a mee)

So, let's go back to our initial dialogue. To begin with, how would you say "I'm going to Spain"?

Voy a España.
(voy a es-pan-ya)

And how would you say "in July"?

en julio
(en hoo-lee-oh)

And again how would you say "because of you" (informal)?

por ti
(por tee)

So, putting this together, how would you say "I'm going to Spain in July because of you" (informal)?

¡Voy a España en julio por ti!
(voy a es-pan-ya en hoo-lee-oh por tee)

And what is "because of me?"

¿Por mí?
(por mee)

So, how would you reply "Because of me? You mean *thanks* to me!" (informal)?

¿Por mí? ¡Quieres decir *gracias* a mí!
(por mee kee-air-es de-seer / de-theer gra-see-ass a mee)

Now, try the entire dialogue below and see how you get on. Take your time and think out each step bit by bit until it all comes naturally and effortlessly. And remember, there's no rush!

I'm going to Spain in July because of you! (informal)
¡Voy a España en julio por ti!
(voy a es-pan-ya en hoo-lee-oh por tee)

Because of me? You mean *thanks* to me! (informal)
¿*Por* mí? ¡Quieres decir *gracias* a mí!
(por mee kee-air-es de-seer / de-theer gra-see-ass a mee)

Building Blocks 7

Some especially useful building blocks this time, I'm sure you'll agree:

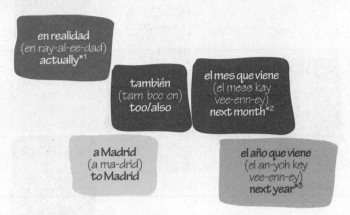

en realidad
(en ray-al-ee-dad)
actually[1]

también
(tam-bee-en)
too/also

el mes que viene
(el mess kay
vee-enn-ey)
next month[2]

a Madrid
(a ma-drid)
to Madrid

el año que viene
(el an-yoh key
vee-enn-ey)
next year[3]

[1] literally "in reality"

[2] literally "the month that comes / is coming"

[3] literally "the year that comes / is coming"

There are four columns on this occasion. More columns of course equal even more fun!

*1 literally "in reality"

*2 literally "the month that comes / is coming"

*3 literally "the year that comes / is coming"

Checklist 7

The penultimate checklist – you're almost there...

el fin de semana (el fin dey sem-arn-er)	the weekend
romántico (roe-man-tick-oh)	romantic
típico (tip-ick-oh)	typical
político (po-li-tick-oh)	political
lógico (lo-hee-koh)	logical
histórico (ee-sto-rick-oh)	historical

crítico (kri-tick-oh)	critical
clásico (clas-ick-oh)	classical
eléctrico (el-ek-trick-oh)	electrical
idéntico (ee-dent-ick-oh)	identical
biológico (hee-oh-lo-hee-koh)	biological
entusiasmado (en-tooz-ee-as-mard-oh)	enthusiastic
Visité (visit-ay)	I visited
Barcelona (bar-sair-loan-er / bar-thair-loan-er)	Barcelona
Madrid (ma-drid)	Madrid
Visité Madrid. (visit-ay ma-drid)	I visited Madrid.
Pasé (pass-ay)	I spent
Pasó (pass-o)	You spent
Pasamos (pass-arm-oss)	We spent
septiembre (sep-tee-em-brey)	September
la Navidad (la na-vee-dad)	Christmas (literally "the Christmas")
en Barcelona (en bar-sair-loan-er / bar-thair-loan-er)	in Barcelona
en España (en es-pan-ya)	in Spain
en México (en me-hee-koe)	in Mexico
Pasamos la Navidad en México. (pass-arm-oss la na-vee-dad en me-hee-koe)	We spent Christmas in Mexico.
Pasó septiembre en España. (pass-o sep-tee-em-brey en es-pan-ya)	You spent September in Spain.
y (ee)	and
fue (fway)	it was
fue romántico (fway roe-man-tick-oh)	it was romantic
adorable (ad-or-arb-lay)	lovely / adorable

fue adorable (fway ad-or-arb-lay)	it was lovely / it was adorable
Pasé el fin de semana en Barcelona... y fue adorable. (pass-ay el fin dey sem-arn-er en bar-sair-loan-er / bar-thair-loan-er ee fway ad-or-arb-lay)	I spent the weekend in Barcelona... and it was lovely.
invitación (in-vit-ass-ee-on)	invitation
Invité (in-vit-ay)	I invited
preparación (pray-par-ass-ee-on)	preparation
Preparé (pre-par-ay)	I prepared
reservación (re-surv-ass-ee-on / re-surv-ath-ee-on)	reservation (preferred in Latin American)
reserva (re-surv-a)	reservation (preferred in Spain)
Reservé (re-surv-ay)	I reserved / booked
cooperación (cope-air-ass-ee-on / cope-air-ath-ee-on)	cooperation
Cooperé (cope-air-ay)	I cooperated
imaginación (im-a-hin-ass-ee-on / im-a-hin-ath-ee-on)	imagination
Imaginé (im-a-hin-ay)	I imagined
manipulación (man-ip-ool-ass-ee-on / man-ip-ool-ath-ee-on)	manipulation
Manipulé (man-ip-ool-ay)	I manipulated
continuación (con-tin-oo-ass-ee-on / con-tin-oo-ath-ee-on)	continuation
Continué (con-tin-oo-ay)	I continued
participación (par-tis-ip-ass-ee-on / par-tith-ip-ath-ee-on)	participation
Participé (par-tis-ip-ay / par-tith-ip-ay)	I participated
exageración (ex-a-hair-ass-ee-on / ex-a-hair-ath-ee-on)	exaggeration
Exageré (ex-a-hair-ay)	I exaggerated
admiración (ad-mi-rass-ee-on / ad-mi-rath-ee-on)	admiration

Admiré (ad-mi-ray)	I admired
irritación (ee-ri-tass-ee-on / ee-ri-tath-ee-on)	irritation
Irrité (ee-ri-tay)	I irritated
conversación (con-vair-sass-ee-on / con-vair-sath-ee-on)	conversation
Conversé (con-vair-say)	I conversed
Ordené (or-den-ay)	I ordered (preferred in Latin American)
Pedí (pe-dee)	I ordered (literally "I asked for") – (preferred in Spain)
Pagué (pag-ay)	I paid
Hice (ee-say / ee-thay)	I did
la cuenta (la kwen-ta)	the bill
la cena (la say-ner / thay-ner)	the dinner
sopa (soap-er)	soup
una mesa (oon-er may-ser)	a table
una habitación (oon-er ab-it-ass-ee-on / ab-it-ath-ee-on)	a room
un taxi (oon taxi)	a taxi
Preparé la cena. (pre-par-ay la say-ner / thay-ner)	I prepared the dinner.
Ordené sopa para la cena. (or-den-ay soap-er pa-ra la say-ner / thay-ner)	I ordered soup for dinner. (preferred in Latin American)
Pedí sopa para la cena. (pe-dee soap-er pa-ra la say-ner / thay-ner)	I ordered soup for dinner. (preferred in Spain)
Reservé una mesa para usted. (re-surv-ay oon-er may-ser pa-ra oo-stedd)	I booked a table for you.
Ella reservó (ay-a re-surv-o)	She booked / reserved
Ella reservó una mesa para esta noche. (ay-a re-surv-ay oon-er may-ser pa-ra es-ta noch-ay)	She booked / reserved a table for this evening.
Él reservó (el re-surv-o)	He booked / reserved

Él reservó una habitación para dos personas. (el re-surv-o oon-er ab-it-ass-ee-on / ab-it-ath-ee-on pa-ra doss pair-so-nass)	He booked / reserved a room for two people.
¿Qué? (kay)	What?
¿Qué preparó? (kay pre-par-o)	What did you prepare?
¿Qué preparó usted? (kay pre-par-o oo-sted)	What did you prepare?
¿Qué hizo usted? (kay ee-soe / ee-thoe oo-sted)	What did you do?
Reservé una mesa, ordené la cena y luego pagué la cuenta. ¿Qué hizo usted? (re-surv-ay oon-er may-ser, or-den-ay la say-ner / thay-ner ee loo-way-go pag-ay la kwen-ta. kay ee-soe / ee-thoe oo-sted)	I booked a table, ordered dinner and then paid the bill. What did you do?
Tengo la intención de… (ten-go la in-ten-see-on / in-ten-thee-on dey)	I'm planning to… (literally "I have the intention of…")
Tengo la intención de volver a España en mayo. (ten-go la in-ten-see-on / in-ten-thee-on dey vol-vair a es-pan-ya en my-oh)	I'm planning to go back to Spain in May.
Tengo miedo de… (ten-go mee-ed-oh dey)	I'm scared of… (literally "I have fear of…")
Tengo miedo de volver a España en septiembre. (ten-go mee-ed-oh dey vol-vair a es-pan-ya en sep-tee-em-brey)	I'm scared of going back to Spain in September.
¿De verdad? (dey vair-dad)	Really?
por lo que (poor-low-kay)	so
pero (pair-o)	but
Tengo ganas de… (ten-go ga-nas dey)	I feel like… / I fancy… (literally "I have desire of…")

Sí, tengo ganas de volver a Barcelona, pero tengo miedo de volar, por lo que tengo la intención de tomar el Eurostar. (see ten-go ga-nas dey vol-vair a bar-sair-loan-er / bar-thair-loan-er pair o ten-go mee-ed-oh dey vol-ar, poor-low-kay ten-go la in-ten-see-on / in-ten-thee-on dey to-mar el e-oo-roe-star)	Yes, I feel like going back to Barcelona but I'm scared of flying, so I'm planning to take the Eurostar.
Tengo ganas de comprar algo esta mañana. (ten-go ga-nas dey com-prar al-go es-ta man-yarn-a)	I feel like / fancy buying something this morning.
Tengo ganas de leer algo esta tarde. (ten-go ga-nas dey lay-air al-go es-ta tar-dey)	I feel like / fancy reading something this afternoon.
Tiene (tee-en-ey)	You have (formal)
Tiene ganas de comer algo esta noche. (tee-en-ey ga-nas dey kom-air al-go es-ta noch-ay)	You feel like eating something this evening. (formal)
Necesito (ness-e-seet-oh / neth-e-seet-oh)	I need
Necesito hablar español. (ness-e-seet-oh / neth-e-seet-oh a-blar es-pa-nyol)	I need to speak Spanish.
Necesito un taxi. (ness-e-seet-oh / neth-e-seet-oh oon taxi)	I need a taxi.
Necesito una habitación. (ness-e-seet-oh / neth-e-seet-oh oon-er ab-it-ass-ee-on / ab-it-ath-ee-on)	I need a room.
Necesito ayuda. (ness-e-seet-oh / neth-e-seet-oh a-yoo-der)	I need help.
¡Necesitas ayuda, camarada! (ness-e-seet-ass / neth-e-seet-ass a-yoo-der ca-ma-ra-da)	You need help, mate!

Odio (oh-dee-oh)	I hate
¡Odio volar! (oh-dee-oh vol-ar)	I hate flying!
Odio vivir con mis suegros. (odio viv-eer kon miss soo-egg-ros)	I hate living with my in-laws.
Odias comer con mis padres. (oh-dee-ass sey-nan-doh kon miss pard-res)	You hate having dinner with my parents. (informal)
Odia trabajar aquí. (oh-dee-a trab-a-har a-key)	You hate working here. (formal)
Estaba (es-tah-bah)	I was
solitario (so-lit-ar-ee-oh)	solitary
contrario (kon-trar-ee-oh)	contrary
ordinario (or-din-ar-ee-oh)	ordinary
Estaba a punto de… (es-tah-bah a poon-toe dey)	I was about to… / I was just about to… (literally "I was at point of…")
Estaba a punto de preparar la cena. (es-tah-bah a poon-toe dey pre-par-ar la say-ner / thay-ner)	I was about to prepare the dinner / I was just about to prepare the dinner.
Estaba a punto de pagar la cuenta. (es-tah-bah a poon-toe dey pag-ar la kwen-ta)	I was about to pay the bill.
Estaba a punto de reservar una mesa. (es-tah-bah a poon-toe dey re-surv-ar oon-er may-ser)	I was just about to book a table.
Me llamaste. (may yah-mah-stay)	You called me / You did call me / You have called me. (informal)
cuando (kwan-doh)	when
Estaba a punto de reservar un taxi cuando me llamaste. (es-tah-bah a poon-toe dey re-surv-ar oon taxi kwan-doh may yah-mah-stay.)	I was just about to book a taxi when you called me.
Estaba a punto de salir cuando sonó el teléfono. (es-tah-bah a poon-toe dey sal-ear kwan-doh sonn-oh el tel-ef-on-oh)	I was about to leave when the telephone rang.

Estaba a punto de telefonearte cuando tocaste a la puerta. (es-tah-bah a poon-toe dey tel-ef-own-ay-ar-tay kwan-doh toe-kas-tey a la pwer-ta)	I was just about to phone you when you knocked at the door. (informal)
Estaba a punto de reservar un taxi cuando comenzó a llover. (es-tah-bah a poon-toe dey re-surv-ar oon taxi kwan-doh emp-ess-oh / emp-eth-oh a yove-air)	I was just about to order a taxi when it started to rain.
Llegaste. (ye-gah-stay)	You have arrived / You arrived / You did arrive. (informal)
Lo siento. (lo see-en-toe)	I'm sorry.
un poco (oon pock-oh)	a little / a bit
Estaba un poco distraído / distraída. (es-tah-bah oon pock-oh dis-tray-doh / dis-tray-da)	I was a little preoccupied / distracted.
Estaba ocupado / ocupada... (es-tah-bah occ-oopa-doh / occ-oopa-da)	I was busy...
Lo siento, estaba ocupado / ocupada cenando cuando llegaste. (lo see-en-toe, es-tah-bah occ-oopa-doh / occ-oopa-da sey-nan-doh kwan-doh ye-gah-stay)	I'm sorry, I was busy having dinner when you arrived. (informal)
Lo siento, estaba ocupado / ocupada preparando la cena cuando llegaste, por lo que estaba un poco distraído / distraída. (lo see-en-toe, es-tah-bah occ-oopa-doh / occ-oopa-da pre-par-ar la say-ner / thay-ner kwan-doh ye-gah-stay poor-low-kee es-tah-bah oon pock-oh dis-tray-doh / dis-tray-da)	I'm sorry, I was busy preparing the dinner when you arrived, so I was a bit distracted. (informal)

Estaba ocupado / ocupada ordenando la casa cuando llegó mi madre. (es-tah-bah occ-oopa-doh / occ-oopa-da or-de-nan-doh la ca-sa kwan-doh yeg-oh mee mar-dray)	I was busy tidying the house when my mother arrived.
Estaba ocupado / ocupada pintando cuando me llamaste. (es-tah-bah occ-oopa-doh / occ-oopa-da peen-tan-doh kwan-doh may yah-mah-stay)	I was busy painting when you called me.
Estaba ocupado / ocupada hablando por teléfono cuando llegó tu carta. (es-tah-bah occ-oopa-doh / occ-oopa-da ah-blan-doh por te-ley-foh-noh kwan-doh yeg-oh too car-ta)	I was busy speaking on the telephone when your letter arrived.
julio (hoo-lee-oh)	July
en julio (en hoo-lee-oh)	in July
Visité Barcelona en julio. (visit-ay bar-sair-loan-er / bar-thair-loan-er en hoo-lee-oh)	I visited Barcelona in July.
Tengo la intención de visitar Barcelona en julio. (ten-go la in-ten-see-on / in-ten-thee-on dey visit-ar bar-sair-loan-er / bar-thair-loan-er)	I'm planning to visit Barcelona in July.
Voy (voy a)	I'm going
Voy a España en septiembre. (voy a es-pan-ya en sep-tee-em-brey)	I'm going to Spain in September.
por... (por)	because of...
por usted (por oo-sted)	because of you (formal)
por ti (por tee)	because of you (informal)
gracias a... (gra-see-ass a)	thanks to...
¡Gracias a mí! (gra-see-ass a mee)	Thanks to me!
¡Voy a España en julio por ti! (voy a es-pan-ya en hoo-lee-oh por tee)	I'm going to Spain in July because of you! (informal)

¿Quieres? (kee-air-es)	Do you want? (literally "want you?") – (informal)
¿Quieres preparar la cena esta noche? (kee-air-es pre-par-ar la say-ner / thay-ner es-ta noch-ay)	Do you want to prepare the dinner this evening? (informal)
¿Quieres comer algo? (koo-air-es sey-nan-doh al-go)	Do you want to eat something? (informal)
Quieres (kee-air-es)	You want (informal)
decir (de-seer / de-theer)	to say
Quieres decir (kee-air-es de-seer / de-theer)	You mean (informal) – (literally "you want to say")
¡Voy a España en julio por ti! (voy a es-pan-ya en hoo-lee-oh por tee)	I'm going to Spain in July because of you! (informal)
¿Por mí? ¡Quieres decir "gracias a mí"! (por mee kee-air-es de-seer / de-theer gra-see-ass a mee)	Because of me? You mean thanks to me! (informal)
En realidad, voy a Madrid también. (en ray-al-ee-dad, voy a ma-drid tam-bee-en)	Actually, I'm going to Madrid too.
En realidad, voy a España el mes que viene. (en ray-al-ee-dad, voy a es-pan-ya el mess kay vee-enn-ey)	Actually, I'm going to Spain next month.
En realidad, voy a Barcelona el año que viene. (en ray-al-ee-dad, voy a bar-sair-loan-er / bar-thair-loan-er el an-yoh kay vee-enn-ey)	Actually, I'm going to Barcelona next year.

Flip-flop time!

the weekend	el fin de semana (el fin dey sem-arn-er)
romantic	romántico (roe-man-tick-oh)
typical	típico (tip-ick-oh)
political	político (po-li-tick-oh)

logical	lógico (lo-hee-koh)
historical	histórico (ee-sto-rick-oh)
critical	crítico (kri-tick-oh)
classical	clásico (clas-ick-oh)
electrical	eléctrico (el-ek-trick-oh)
identical	idéntico (ee-dent-ick-oh)
biological	biológico (bee-oh-lo-hee-koh)
enthusiastic	entusiasmado (en-tooz-ee-as-mard-oh)
I visited	Visité (visit-ay)
Barcelona	Barcelona (bar-sair-loan-er / bar-thair-loan-er)
Madrid	Madrid (ma-drid)
I visited Madrid.	Visité Madrid. (visit-ay ma-drid)
I spent	Pasé (pass-ay)
You spent	Pasó (pass-o)
We spent	Pasamos (pass-arm-oss)
September	septiembre (sep-tee-em-brey)
Christmas (literally "the Christmas")	la Navidad (la na-vee-dad)
in Barcelona	en Barcelona (en bar-sair-loan-er / bar-thair-loan-er)
in Spain	en España (en es-pan-ya)
in Mexico	en México (en me-hee-koe)
We spent Christmas in Mexico.	Pasamos la Navidad en México. (pass-arm-oss la na-vee-dad en me-hee-koe)
You spent September in Spain.	Pasó septiembre en España. (pass-o sep-tee-em-brey en es-pan-ya)
and	y (ee)
it was	fue (fway)
it was romantic	fue romántico (fway roe-man-tick-oh)

lovely / adorable	adorable (ad-or-arb-lay)
it was lovely / it was adorable	fue adorable (fway ad-or-arb-lay)
I spent the weekend in Barcelona... and it was lovely.	Pasé el fin de semana en Barcelona... y fue adorable. (pass-ay el fin dey sem-arn-er en bar-sair-loan-er / bar-thair-loan-er ee fway ad-or-arb-lay)
invitation	invitación (in-vit-ass-ee-on)
I invited	Invité (in-vit-ay)
preparation	preparación (pray-par-ass-ee-on)
I prepared	Preparé (pre-par-ay)
reservation (preferred in Latin American)	reservación (re-surv-ass-ee-on / re-surv-ath-ee-on)
reservation (preferred in Spain)	reserva (re-surv-a)
I reserved / booked	Reservé (re-surv-ay)
cooperation	cooperación (cope-air-ass-ee-on / cope-air-ath-ee-on)
I cooperated	Cooperé (cope-air-ay)
imagination	imaginación (im-a-hin-ass-ee-on / im-a-hin-ath-ee-on)
I imagined	Imaginé (im-a-hin-ay)
manipulation	manipulación (man-ip-ool-ass-ee-on / man-ip-ool-ath-ee-on)
I manipulated	Manipulé (man-ip-ool-ay)
continuation	continuación (con-tin-oo-ass-ee-on / con-tin-oo-ath-ee-on)
I continued	Continué (con-tin-oo-ay)
participation	participación (par-tis-ip-ass-ee-on / par-tith-ip-ath-ee-on)
I participated	Participé (par-tis-ip-ay / par-tith-ip-ay)
exaggeration	exageración (ex-a-hair-ass-ee-on / ex-a-hair-ath-ee-on)
I exaggerated	Exageré (ex-a-hair-ay)

admiration	admiración (ad-mi-rass-ee-on / ad-mi-rath-ee-on)
I admired	Admiré (ad-mi-ray)
irritation	irritación (ee-ri-tass-ee-on / ee-ri-tath-ee-on)
I irritated	Irrité (ee-ri-tay)
conversation	conversación (con-vair-sass-ee-on / con-vair-sath-ee-on)
I conversed	Conversé (con-vair-say)
I ordered (preferred in Latin American)	Ordené (or-den-ay)
I ordered (literally "I asked for") – (preferred in Spain)	Pedí (pe-dee)
I paid	Pagué (pag-ay)
I did	Hice (ee-say / ee-thay)
the bill	la cuenta (la kwon-ta)
the dinner	la cena (la say-ner / thay-ner)
soup	sopa (soap-er)
a table	una mesa (oon-er may-ser)
a room	una habitación (oon-er ab-it-ass-ee-on / ab-it-ath-ee-on)
a taxi	un taxi (oon taxi)
I prepared the dinner.	Preparé la cena. (pre-par-ay la say-ner / thay-ner)
I ordered soup for dinner. (preferred in Latin American)	Ordené sopa para la cena. (or-den-ay soap-er pa-ra la say-ner / thay-ner)
I ordered soup for dinner. (preferred in Spain)	Pedí sopa para la cena. (pe-dee soap-er pa-ra la say-ner / thay-ner)
I booked a table for you.	Reservé una mesa para usted. (re-surv-ay oon-er may-ser pa-ra oo-stedd)
She booked / reserved	Ella reservó (ay-a re-surv-o)
She booked / reserved a table for this evening.	Ella reservó una mesa para esta noche. (ay-a re-surv-ay oon-er may-ser pa-ra es-ta noch-ay)

He booked / reserved	Él reservó (el re-surv-o)
He booked / reserved a room for two people.	Él reservó una habitación para dos personas. (el re-surv-o oon-er ab-it-ass-ee-on / ab-it-ath-ee-on pa-ra doss pair-so-nass)
What?	¿Qué? (kay)
What did you prepare?	¿Qué preparó? (kay pre-par-o)
What did you prepare?	¿Qué preparó usted? (kay pre-par-o oo-sted)
What did you do?	¿Qué hizo usted? (kay ee-soe / ee-thoe oo-sted)
I booked a table, ordered dinner and then paid the bill. What did you do?	Reservé una mesa, ordené la cena y luego pagué la cuenta. ¿Qué hizo usted? (re-surv-ay oon-er may-ser, or-den-ay la say-ner / thay-ner ee loo-way-go pag-ay la kwen-ta. kay ee-soe / ee-thoe oo-sted)
I'm planning to... (literally "I have the intention of...")	Tengo la intención de... (ten-go la in-ten-see-on / in-ten-thee-on dey)
I'm planning to go back to Spain in May.	Tengo la intención de volver a España en mayo. (ten-go la in-ten-see-on / in-ten-thee-on dey vol-vair a es-pan-ya en my-oh)
I'm scared of... (literally "I have fear of...")	Tengo miedo de... (ten-go mee-ed-oh dey)
I'm scared of going back to Spain in September.	Tengo miedo de volver a España en septiembre. (ten-go mee-ed-oh dey vol-vair a es-pan-ya en sep-tee-em-brey)
Really?	¿De verdad? (dey vair-dad)
so	por lo que (poor-low-kay)
but	pero (pair-o)
I feel like... / I fancy... (literally "I have desire of...")	Tengo ganas de... (ten-go ga-nas dey)

Yes, I feel like going back to Barcelona but I'm scared of flying, so I'm planning to take the Eurostar.	Sí, tengo ganas de volver a Barcelona, pero tengo miedo de volar, por lo que tengo la intención de tomar el Eurostar. (see ten-go ga-nas dey vol-vair a bar-sair-loan-er / bar-thair-loan-er pair-o ten-go mee-ed-oh dey vol-ar, poor-low-kay ten-go la in-ten-see-on / in-ten-thee-on dey to-mar el e-oo-roe-star)
I feel like / fancy buying something this morning.	Tengo ganas de comprar algo esta mañana. (ten-go ga-nas dey com-prar al-go es-ta man-yarn-a)
I feel like / fancy reading something this afternoon.	Tengo ganas de leer algo esta tarde. (ten-go ga-nas dey lay-air al-go es-ta tar-dey)
You have (formal)	Tiene (tee-en-ey)
You feel like eating something this evening. (formal)	Tiene ganas de comer algo esta noche. (tee-en-ey ga-nas dey kom-air al-go es-ta noch-ay)
I need	Necesito (ness-e-seet-oh / neth-e-seet-oh)
I need to speak Spanish.	Necesito hablar español. (ness-e-seet-oh / neth-e-seet-oh a-blar es-pa-nyol)
I need a taxi.	Necesito un taxi. (ness-e-seet-oh / neth-e-seet-oh oon taxi)
I need a room.	Necesito una habitación. (ness-e-seet-oh / neth-e-seet-oh oon-er ab-it-ass-ee-on / ab-it-ath-ee-on)
I need help.	Necesito ayuda. (ness-e-seet-oh / neth-e-seet-oh a-yoo-der)
You need help, mate!	¡Necesitas ayuda, camarada! (ness-e-seet-ass / neth-e-seet-ass a-yoo-der ca-ma-ra-da)
I hate	Odio (oh-dee-oh)
I hate flying!	¡Odio volar! (oh-dee-oh vol-ar)

I hate living with my in-laws.	Odio vivir con mis suegros. (odio viv-eer kon miss soo-egg-ros)
You hate having dinner with my parents. (informal)	Odias comer con mis padres. (oh-dee-ass sey-nan-doh kon miss pard-res)
You hate working here. (formal)	Odia trabajar aquí. (oh-dee-a trab-a-har a-key)
I was	Estaba (es-tah-bah)
solitary	solitario (so-lit-ar-ee-oh)
contrary	contrario (kon-trar-ee-oh)
ordinary	ordinario (or-din-ar-ee-oh)
I was about to… / I was just about to… (literally "I was at point of…")	Estaba a punto de… (es-tah-bah a poon-toe dey)
I was about to prepare the dinner / I was just about to prepare the dinner.	Estaba a punto de preparar la cena. (es-tah-bah a poon-toe dey pre-par-ar la say-ner / thay-ner)
I was about to pay the bill.	Estaba a punto de pagar la cuenta. (es-tah-bah a poon-toe dey pag-ar la kwen-ta)
I was just about to book a table.	Estaba a punto de reservar una mesa. (es-tah-bah a poon-toe dey re-surv-ar oon-er may-ser)
You called me / You did call me / You have called me. (informal)	Me llamaste. (may yah-mah-stay)
when	cuando (kwan-doh)
I was just about to book a taxi when you called me.	Estaba a punto de reservar un taxi cuando me llamaste. (es-tah-bah a poon-toe dey re-surv-ar oon taxi kwan-doh may yah-mah-stay.)
I was about to leave when the telephone rang.	Estaba a punto de salir cuando sonó el teléfono. (es-tah-bah a poon-toe dey sal-ear kwan-doh sonn-oh el tel-ef-on-oh)

I was just about to phone you when you knocked at the door. (informal)	Estaba a punto de telefonearte cuando tocaste a la puerta. (es-tah-bah a poon-toe dey tel-ef-own-ay-ar-tay kwan-doh toe-kas-tey a la pwer-ta)
I was just about to order a taxi when it started (literally "commenced") to rain.	Estaba a punto de reservar un taxi cuando comenzó a llover. (es-tah-bah a poon-toe dey re-surv-ar oon taxi kwan-doh emp-ess-oh / emp-eth-oh a yove-air)
You have arrived / You arrived / You did arrive. (informal)	Llegaste. (ye-gah-stay)
I'm sorry.	Lo siento. (lo see-en-toe)
a little / a bit	un poco (oon pock-oh)
I was a little preoccupied / distracted.	Estaba un poco distraído / distraída. (es-tah-bah oon pock-oh dis-tray-doh / dis-tray-da)
I was busy…	Estaba ocupado / ocupada… (es-tah-bah occ-oopa-doh / occ-oopa-da)
I'm sorry, I was busy having dinner when you arrived. (informal)	Lo siento, estaba ocupado / ocupada cenando cuando llegaste. (lo see-en-toe, es-tah-bah occ-oopa-doh / occ-oopa-da sey-nan-doh kwan-doh ye-gah-stay)
I'm sorry, I was busy preparing the dinner when you arrived, so I was a bit distracted. (informal)	Lo siento, estaba ocupado / ocupada preparando la cena cuando llegaste, por lo que estaba un poco distraído / distraída. (lo see-en-toe, es-tah-bah occ-oopa-doh / occ-oopa-da pre-par-ar la say-ner / thay-ner kwan-doh ye-gah-stay poor-low-kee es-tah-bah oon pock-oh dis-tray-doh / dis-tray-da)
I was busy tidying the house when my mother arrived.	Estaba ocupado / ocupada ordenando la casa cuando llegó mi madre. (es-tah-bah occ-oopa-doh / occ-oopa-da or-de-nan-doh la ca-sa kwan-doh yeg-oh mee mar-dray)

I was busy painting when you called me.	Estaba ocupado / ocupada pintando cuando me llamaste. (es-tah-bah occ-oopa-doh / occ-oopa-da peen-tan-doh kwan-doh may yah-mah-stay)
I was busy speaking on the telephone when your letter arrived.	Estaba ocupado / ocupada hablando por teléfono cuando llegó tu carta. (es-tah-bah occ-oopa-doh / occ-oopa-da ah-blan-doh por te-ley-foh-noh kwan-doh yeg-oh too car-ta)
July	julio (hoo-lee-oh)
in July	en julio (en hoo-lee-oh)
I visited Barcelona in July.	Visité Barcelona en julio. (visit-ay bar-sair-loan-er / bar-thair-loan-er en hoo-lee-oh)
I'm planning to visit Barcelona in July.	Tengo la intención de visitar Barcelona en julio. (ten-go la in-ten-see-on / in-ten-thee-on dey visit-ar bar-sair-loan-er / bar-thair-loan-er)
I'm going	Voy (voy a)
I'm going to Spain in September.	Voy a España en septiembre. (voy a es-pan-ya en sep-tee-em-brey)
because of…	por… (por)
because of you (formal)	por usted (por oo-sted)
because of you (informal)	por ti (por tee)
thanks to…	gracias a… (gra-see-ass a)
Thanks to me!	¡Gracias a mí! (gra-see-ass a mee)
I'm going to Spain in July because of you! (informal)	¡Voy a España en julio por ti! (voy a es-pan-ya en hoo-lee-oh por tee)
Do you want? (literally "want you?") – (informal)	¿Quieres? (kee-air-es)
Do you want to prepare the dinner this evening? (informal)	¿Quieres preparar la cena esta noche? (kee-air-es pre-par-ar la say-ner / thay-ner es-ta noch-ay)

Do you want to eat something? (informal)	¿Quieres comer algo? (kee-air-es sey-nan-doh al-go)
You want (informal)	Quieres (kee-air-es)
to say	decir (de-seer / de-theer)
You mean (literally "you want to say") – (informal)	Quieres decir (kee-air-es de-seer / de-theer)
I'm going to Spain in July because of you! (informal)	¡Voy a España en julio por ti! (voy a es-pan-ya en hoo-lee-oh por tee)
Because of me? You mean thanks to me! (informal)	¿Por mí? ¡Quieres decir "gracias a mí"! (por mee kee-air-es de-seer / de-theer gra-see-ass a mee)
Actually, I'm going to Madrid too.	En realidad, voy a Madrid también. (en ray-al-ee-dad, voy a ma-drid tam-bee-en)
Actually, I'm going to Spain next month.	En realidad, voy a España el mes que viene. (en ray-al-ee-dad, voy a es-pan-ya el mess kay vee-enn-ey)
Actually, I'm going to Barcelona next year.	En realidad, voy a Barcelona el año que viene. (en ray-al-ee-dad, voy a bar-sair-loan-er / bar-thair-loan-er el an-yoh kay vee-enn-ey)

And it's done! Take a break now before you dive into the final chapter!

Between Chapters Tip!

The Great Word Robbery

Since the very beginning of the book, I've been giving you examples of how you can rapidly build up your Spanish vocabulary by stealing and converting words from English. Really though, what I've shown you so far has only been the tip of that enormous iceberg I mentioned in the Introduction.

Below, I'm going to give you a far more comprehensive list of word endings that you can use to create thousands of words in Spanish.

Once you've had a read through them, I recommend that you try coming up with a few more examples for each, saying them out loud. The more you do this the more you will find yourself able to apply the various conversion techniques between English and Spanish almost instinctively.

So, here is the list – it will be your single greatest aid in increasing your Spanish vocabulary:

Words ending in . . . in English	Usually become . . . in Spanish	Examples
ation	ación	decoración preparación transformación **(1250)**
ic/ical	ico	político típico dramático **(750)**
ary	ario	primario salario voluntario **(400)**
ous	oso	curioso furioso religioso **(400)**
ade	ada	barricada década cascada **(150)**
ude	ud	gratitud aptitud altitud **(100)**
ure	ura	agricultura caricatura textura **(300)**

Words ending in . . . in English	Usually become . . . in Spanish	Examples
ible	stay the same	terrible visible flexible **(800)**
able	stay the same	miserable usable probable **(800)**
ant	ante	importante elegante galante **(700)**
ent	ente	presidente cliente reciente **(700)**
id	ido	vívido rápido tímido **(300)**
sm	smo	pesimismo pacifismo sarcasmo **(800)**
ty	dad	realidad atrocidad agilidad **(1500)**
or	stay the same	doctor actor pastor **(800)**

Words ending in . . . in English	Usually become . . . in Spanish	Examples
ist	ista	artista pianista fascista **(1000)**
al	stay the same	local personal central **(200)**
ive	ivo	creativo activo explosivo **(750)**

Word Robbery Total : 12,000

Wow, 12,000 English words that have close relatives in Spanish. Not too shabby in my opinion.

I recommend returning to the list every so often to practise stealing words via the conversion techniques. Try to come up with a couple of examples for each and then check them in a dictionary as a way to learn any exceptions to the rules given above.

CHAPTER 8

When you talk
about Barcelona,
you sound
so enthusiastic.

When you talk about Barcelona, you sound so enthusiastic.

Well, you've worked through seven chapters to get to this point. I think it's time to see what you're capable of saying based on all you've learnt with the book.

You are therefore going to now build up to a much longer dialogue than you've done previously *but* much of what you're building towards you will already be familiar with.

Now, I am sure that you can definitely do this, so let's begin.

What is "I have visited", "I visited", "I did visit"?

Visité
(visit-ay)

How about "I have reserved / booked", "I reserved / booked", "I did reserve / book"?

Reservé
(re-surv-ay)

"I have prepared", "I prepared", "I did prepare"?

Preparé
(pre-par-ay)

"I have ordered", "I ordered", "I did order"?

Ordené
(or-den-ay)

"I have paid", "I paid", "I did pay"?

Pagué
(pag-ay)

"I have spent", "I spent", "I did spend"?

Pasé
(pass-ay)

And how would you say "I spent the weekend in Spain"?

Pasé el fin de semana en España.
(pass-ay el fin dey sem-arn-er en es-pan-ya)

And how would you say "it was" in Spanish?

Fue
(fway)

And so how would you say "it was lovely"?

Fue adorable.
(fway ad-or-arb-lay)

And what was the word for "and" in Spanish?

y
(ee)

So how would you say "I spent the weekend in Spain and it was lovely"?

Pasé el fin de semana en España y fue adorable.
(pass-ay el fin dey sem-arn-er en es-pan-ya ee fway ad-or-arb-lay)

And how would you say "I'm planning to..." in Spanish?

Tengo la intención de...
(ten-go la in-ten-see-on / in-ten-thee-on dey)

So how would you say "I'm planing to go back to Barcelona in May"?

Tengo la intención de volver a Barcelona en mayo.
(ten-go la in-ten-see-on / in-ten-thee-on dey vol-vair a bar-sair-loan-er /
bar-thair-loan-er en my-oh)

Now, let's put those two bits together and say "I spent the weekend in Spain and it was lovely. I'm planning to go back to Barcelona in May".

Pasé el fin de semana en España y fue adorable. Tengo la intención de volver a Barcelona en mayo.
(pass-ay el fin dey sem-arn-er en es-pan-ya ee fway ad-or-arb-lay. ten-go la in-ten-see-on / in-ten-thee-on dey vol-vair a bar-sair-loan-er / bar-thair-loan-er en my-oh)

Now again, what is "I have"?

Tengo
(ten-go)

And "you have" (formal)?

Tiene
(tee-en-ey)

What about "you have" (informal)?

Tienes
(tee-en-es)

So how would you say "you are planning to..." (informal)?

Tienes la intención de...
(tee-en-es la in-ten-see-on / in-ten-thee-on dey)

And how would you say "you're scared of..." (informal)?

Tienes miedo de...
(tee-en-es mee-ed-oh dey)

How about "you're scared of flying" (informal)?

Tienes miedo de volar.
(tee-en-es mee-ed-oh dey vol-ar)

216

What is "but"?

pero
(pair-o)

So how would you say "But you're scared of flying!"?

¡Pero tienes miedo de volar!
(pair-o tee-en-es mee-ed-oh dey vol-ar)

What is "to take"?

tomar
(to-mar)

How would you say "I'm planning to take the Eurostar"?

Tengo la intención de tomar el Eurostar.
(ten-go la in-ten-see-on / in-ten-thee-on dey to-mar el e-oo-roe-star)

What is "so" in Spanish?

por lo que
(poor-low-kay)

Knowing that, how would you say "so I'm planning to take the Eurostar"?

por lo que tengo la intención de tomar el Eurostar
(poor-low-kay ten-go la in-ten-see-on / in-ten-thee-on dey to-mar el
e-oo-roe-star)

And again, what is "I'm planning to..."?

Tengo la intención de...
(ten-go la in-ten-see-on / in-ten-thee-on dey)

And what is "I'm scared of..."?

Tengo miedo de...
(ten-go mee-ed-oh dey)

What about "I hate"?

Odio
(oh-dee-oh)

So how would you say "I hate the Eurostar"?

Odio el Eurostar.
(oh-dee-oh el e-oo-roe-star)

What is "really"?

de verdad
(dey vair-dad)

So how would you say "Really? I hate the Eurostar!"

¿De verdad? ¡Odio el Eurostar!
(dey vair-dad odio el e-oo-roe-star)

What is "I need"?

Necesito
(ness-e-seet-oh / neth-e-seet-oh)

And what is "you need" (formal)?

Necesita
(ness-e-seet-a / neth-e-seet-a)

And how about "you need" (informal)?

Necesitas
(ness-e-seet-ass / neth-e-seet-ass)

So, how would you say "you need help, mate!" (informal)?

¡Necesitas ayuda, camarada!
(ness-e-seet-ass / neth-e-seet-ass a-yoo-der ca-ma-ra-da)

"Great" or "excellent" in Spanish is:

excelente
(ex-se-lent-ey / ex-the-lent-ey)

Okay, how would you say "the Eurostar is great / excellent"?

El Eurostar es excelente.
(el e-oo-roe-star es ex-se-lent-ey / ex-the-lent-ey)

What is "but"?

pero
(pair-o)

So how would you say "but the Eurostar is great / excellent!"

¡Pero el Eurostar es excelente!
(pair-o el e-oo-roe-star es ex-se-lent-ey / ex-the-lent-ey)

What is "I was just about to..."?

Estaba a punto de...
(es-tah-bah a poon-toe dey)

And "I was just about to book a table"?

Estaba a punto de reservar una mesa.
(es-tah-bah a poon-toe dey re-surv-ar oon-er may-ser)

How about "I was just about to book a taxi"?

Estaba a punto de reservar un taxi.
(es-tah-bah a poon-toe dey re-surv-ar oon taxi)

"I was just about to book a room"?

Estaba a punto de reservar una habitación.
(es-tah-bah a poon-toe dey re-surv-ar oon-er ab-it-ass-ee-on / ab-it-ath-ee-on)

"A ticket" in Spanish is:

un billete
(oon bee-yet-ey)

How would you say "I was just about to book a ticket"?

Estaba a punto de reservar un billete.
(es-tah-bah a poon-toe dey re-surv-ar oon bee-yet-ey)

What is the word for "and"?

y
(ee)

So how would you say "...and I was just about to book a ticket"?

...y estaba a punto de reservar un billete
(ee es-tah-bah a poon-toe dey re-surv-ar oon bee-yet-ey)

And how you would you say "you arrived" in Spanish (informal)?

Llegaste
(ye-gah-stay)

And so how would you say "...when you arrived" (informal)?

...cuando llegaste
(kwan-doh ye-gah-stay)

Put these various parts together now and say "...and I was just about to book a ticket when you arrived."

...y estaba a punto de reservar un billete cuando llegaste.
(ee es-tah-bah a poon-toe dey re-surv-ar oon bee-yet-ey kwan-doh ye-gah-stay)

And now let's put both this and the other parts that came before it together.

Taking your time, say: "But the Eurostar is excellent! – and I was just about to book a ticket when you arrived."

¡Pero el Eurostar es excelente! – y estaba a punto de reservar un billete cuando llegaste.
(pair-o el e-oo-roe-star es ex-se-lent-ey / ex-the-lent-ey ee es-tah-bah a poon-toe dey re-surv-ar oon bee-yet-ey kwan-doh ye-gah-stay)

Now, how would someone respond to that by saying "Really?"

¿De verdad?
(dey vair-dad)

And once more, what is "I was just about to…"?

Estaba a punto de…
(es-tah-bah a poon-toe dey)

And how would you say "I was busy…"?

Estaba ocupado / ocupada…
(es-tah-bah occ-oopa-doh / occ-oopa-da)

So, how would you say "I was busy booking a ticket"?

Estaba ocupado / ocupada reservando un billete.
(es-tah-bah occ-oopa-doh / occ-oopa-da re-surv-and-oh oon bee-yet-ey)

And how would you say "…when you knocked at the door" (informal)?

…cuando tocaste a la puerta
(kwan-doh toe-kas-tey a la pwer-ta)

Now, let's combine these elements and say "I was busy booking a ticket when you knocked at the door."

Estaba ocupado/ ocupada reservando un billete cuando tocaste a la puerta.
(es-tah-bah occ-oopa-doh / occ-oopa-da re-surv-an- doh oon bee-yet-ey kwan-doh toe-kas-tey a la pwer-ta)

"Oh", as in "oh, sorry" in Spanish is:

ay
(eye[14])

So, how would you reply to the previous sentence, saying simply "oh, sorry"?

Ay, lo siento.
(eye lo see-en-toe)

What is "I feel like..." or "I fancy..."?

Tengo ganas de...
(ten-go ga-nas dey)

How about "I feel like visiting Barcelona"?

Tengo ganas de visitar Barcelona.
(ten-go ga-nas dey visit-ar bar-sair-loan-er / bar-thair-loan-er)

What is "too" or "also" in Spanish?

también
(tam-bee-en)

So how would you say "I feel like visiting Barcelona too"?

Tengo ganas de visitar Barcelona también.
(ten-go ga-nas dey visit-ar bar-sair-loan-er / bar-thair-loan-er tam-bee-en)

What is "actually" or "in fact" in Spanish?

en realidad
(en ray-al-ee-dad)

So, giving a fuller answer, how would you say "Oh, sorry. Actually, I feel like visiting Barcelona too."?

Ay, lo siento. En realidad, tengo ganas de visitar Barcelona también.
(eye lo see-en-toe. en ray-al-ee-dad ten-go ga-nas dey visit-ar bar-sair-loan-er / bar-thair-loan-er tam-bee-en)

---

14 Just to make this clear, "ay" is pronounced just like the English word "eye".

How would someone reply to that by saying "Really?"

¿De verdad?
(dey vair-dad)

What is "because of..."?

por...
(por)

And how would you say "because of you" (formal)?

por usted
(por oo-sted)

And how about "because of me"?

por mí
(por mee)

And what about "because of you" (informal)?

por ti
(por tee)

What is "to speak" or "to talk" in Spanish?

hablar
(a-blar)

"You speak" or "you talk" (informal) in Spanish is:

hablas
(ab-lass)

To say "you speak about" or "you talk about" (informal) in Spanish, you will literally say "you speak of" or "you talk of".

hablas de
(ab-lass dey)

So how would you say "you talk about Barcelona" (informal)?

Hablas de Barcelona.
(ab-lass dey bar-sair-loan-er / bar-thair-loan-er)

How about "when you talk about Barcelona" (informal)?

cuando hablas de Barcelona
(kwan-doh ab-lass dey bar-sair-loan-er / bar-thair-loan-er)

"You sound" (informal) in Spanish is:

suenas
(swen-ass)

And what was "enthusiastic" in Spanish?

entusiasmado
(en-tooz-ee-as-mard-oh)

So how would you say "you sound enthusiastic"?

Suenas entusiasmado.
(swen-ass en-tooz-ee-as-mard-oh)

What is "so" in Spanish?

por lo que
(poor-low-kay)

Now, it's worth pointing out that in English we actually use "so" to mean more than one thing. For instance, we can say "I liked the jacket, so I bought it" or "I'm not happy here, so I'm leaving." It's sort of a less formal way of saying "therefore" – "I like the jacket, therefore I bought it", "I'm not happy here, therefore I'm leaving." (It would, of course, sound a bit strange to actually use "therefore" in these situations because it's somewhat formal – but the meaning is essentially the same.)

Anyway, this is the type of "so" that we have been using "por lo que" to express in Spanish, the "so" that is a less formal way of saying "therefore". This is the kind of "so" you would use in the examples I've just given, or to say something like "I'm tired, so I'm going to bed."

There is, however, another way in which we use "so" in English. For instance, when we say "I was so happy", "I was so excited", "he's so romantic!" This "so" clearly isn't the same as the "therefore" we have been using so far. Its meaning is more like "very" or "extremely".

The word for this type of "so" in Spanish is:

tan
(tan)

So how would you say "you sound so enthusiastic" (informal)?

Suenas tan entusiasmado.
(swen-ass tan en-tooz-ee-as-mard-oh)

If you want to reply to something you feel is a compliment you can, of course, say "thank you", which is:

gracias
(gra-see-ass)

If you want to make that more emphatic, you can say "wow, thank you!" "Wow" in Spanish is:

uy
(oy)

So, how would you say "wow, thank you!"?

¡Uy, gracias!
(oy gra-see-ass)

Once again, what is "you speak" or "you talk" (informal) in Spanish?

hablas
(ab-lass)

And how would you say "you speak about" or "you talk about" (informal) – literally "you speak of / you talk of"?

hablas de
(ab-lass dey)

How would you you say "you talk about Barcelona" (informal)?

Hablas de Barcelona.
(ab-lass dey bar-sair-loan-er / bar-thair-loan-er)

And what about "when you talk about Barcelona" (informal)?

cuando hablas de Barcelona
(kwan-doh ab-lass dey bar-sair-loan-er / bar-thair-loan-er)

And again, how would you say "you sound so enthusiastic" (informal)?

Suenas tan entusiasmado.
(swen-ass tan en-tooz-ee-as-mard-oh)

So now, putting this all together, say "When you talk about Barcelona, you sound so enthusiastic."

Cuando hablas de Barcelona, suenas tan entusiasmado.
(kwan-doh ab-lass dey bar-sair-loan-er / bar-thair-loan-er swen-ass tan en-tooz-ee-as-mard-oh)

How would the person you were talking to reply "Wow, thanks!"?

¡Uy, gracias!
(oy, gra-see-ass)

If, by your enthusiasm, you actually managed to persuade someone that they also wanted to go to Barcelona, they might say "Wow, thanks, let's go then!"

"Let's go then!" is:

¡Vamos entonces!
(var-mos en-ton-sess / en-ton-thess)

So, finally, how would you say "Wow, thanks! Let's go then!"?

¡Uy, gracias! ¡Vamos entonces!
(oy gra-see-ass. var-mos en-ton-sess / en-ton-thess)

Alright, I think it's time for you to have a crack at the long dialogue I mentioned at the beginning of the chapter.

Try going through it slowly the first couple of times and then, once you feel confident enough, see if you can get to the point where you can construct the entire dialogue without needing to pause. It will take a fair amount of practice but, every time you go through it, it will greatly benefit your Spanish.

As you will already be finding, I hope, the more you practise constructing these sentences, the more natural and fluent you will sound.

Are you ready then? Take your time and off you go with the final dialogue:

I spent the weekend in Spain and it was lovely. I'm planning to go back to Barcelona in May.
Pasé el fin de semana en España y fue adorable. Tengo la intención de volver a Barcelona en mayo.
(pass-ay el fin dey sem-arn-er en es-pan-ya ee fway ad-or-arb-lay. ten-go la in-ten-see-on / in-ten-thee-on dey vol-vair a bar-sair-loan-er / bar-thair-loan-er en my-oh)

But you're scared of flying!
¡Pero tienes miedo de volar!
(pair-o tee-en-es mee-ed-oh dey vol-ar)

Yes, so I'm planning to take the Eurostar.
Sí, por lo que tengo la intención de tomar el Eurostar.
(see, poor-low-kay ten-go la in-ten-see-on / in-ten-thee-on dey to-mar el e-oo-roe-star)

Really? I hate the Eurostar.
¿De verdad? ¡Odio el Eurostar!
(dey vair-dad oh-dee-oh el e-oo-roe-star)

But the Eurostar is excellent! – and I was just about to book a ticket when you arrived.
¡Pero el Eurostar es excelente! - y estaba a punto de reservar un billete cuando llegaste.
(pair-o el e-oo-roe-star es ex-se-lent-ey / ex-the-lent-ey ee es-tah-bah a poon-toe dey re-surv-ar oon bee-yet-ey kwan-doh ye-gah-stay)

Really?
¿De verdad?
(dey vair-dad)

Yes, I was busy booking a ticket when you knocked at the door.
Sí, estaba ocupado / ocupada reservando un billete cuando tocaste a la puerta.
(see, es-tah-bah occ-oopa-doh / occ-oopa-da re-surv-an-doh oon bee-yet-ey kwan-doh toe-kas-tey a la pwer-ta)

Oh, sorry. Actually, I feel like visiting Barcelona too.
Ay, lo siento. En realidad, tengo ganas de visitar Barcelona también.
(eye lo see-en-toe. en ray-al-ee-dad ten-go ga-nas dey visit-ar bar-sair-loan-er / bar-thair-loan-er tam-bee-en)

Really?
¿De verdad?
(dey vair-dad)

Yes – because of you.
Sí, por ti.
(see, por tee)

Because of me? Really?
¿Por mí? ¿De verdad?
(por mee? dey vair-dad)

Yes, when you talk about Barcelona, you sound so enthusiastic.
Sí, cuando hablas de Barcelona suenas tan entusiasmado.
(see, kwan-doh ab-lass dey bar-sair-loan-er / bar-thair-loan-er swen-ass tan en-tooz-ee-as-mard-oh)

Wow, thanks! Let's go then!
¡Uy, gracias! ¡Vamos entonces!
(oy gra-see-ass. var-mos en-ton-sess / en-ton-thess)

Well, this is your final checklist. Unlike the ones that came before it, however, you are not finished with this one until you can go the whole way through it without making a single mistake.

This doesn't mean that making mistakes when you go through it is a bad thing It's just that I want you to return to it multiple times until going through the list becomes so easy that you can do so without making a single error.

When you can, it means you have really learnt what I wanted to teach you in these pages.

Now, get to it!

el fin de semana (el fin dey sem-arn-er)	the weekend
romántico (roe-man-tick-oh)	romantic
típico (tip-ick-oh)	typical
político (po-li-tick-oh)	political
lógico (lo-hee-koh)	logical
histórico (ee-sto-rick-oh)	historical
crítico (kri-tick-oh)	critical
clásico (clas-ick-oh)	classical
eléctrico (el-ek-trick-oh)	electrical
idéntico (ee-dent-ick-oh)	identical
biológico (bee-oh-lo-hee-koh)	biological
entusiasmado (en-tooz-ee-as-mard-oh)	enthusiastic
Visité (visit-ay)	I visited
Barcelona (bar-sair-loan-er / bar-thair-loan-er)	Barcelona
Madrid (ma-drid)	Madrid
Visité Madrid. (visit-ay ma-drid)	I visited Madrid.

Pasé (pass-ay)	I spent
Pasó (pass-o)	You spent
Pasamos (pass-arm-oss)	We spent
septiembre (sep-tee-em-brey)	September
la Navidad (la na-vee-dad)	Christmas (literally "the Christmas")
en Barcelona (en bar-sair-loan-er / bár-thair-loan-er)	in Barcelona
en España (en es-pan-ya)	in Spain
en México (en me-hee-koe)	in Mexico
Pasamos la Navidad en México. (pass-arm-oss la na-vee-dad en me-hee-koe)	We spent Christmas in Mexico.
Pasó septiembre en España. (pass-o sep-tee-em-brey en es-pan-ya)	You spent September in Spain.
y (ee)	and
fue (fway)	it was
fue romántico (fway roe-man-tick-oh)	it was romantic
adorable (ad-or-arb-lay)	lovely / adorable
fue adorable (fway ad-or-arb-lay)	it was lovely / it was adorable
Pasé el fin de semana en Barcelona... y fue adorable. (pass-ay el fin dey sem-arn-er en bar-sair-loan-er / bar-thair-loan-er ee fway ad-or-arb-lay)	I spent the weekend in Barcelona... and it was lovely.
invitación (in-vit-ass-ee-on)	invitation
Invité (in-vit-ay)	I invited
preparación (pray-par-ass-ee-on)	preparation
Preparé (pre-par-ay)	I prepared
reservación (re-surv-ass-ee-on / re-surv-ath-ee-on)	reservation (preferred in Latin American)
reserva (re-surv-a)	reservation (preferred in Spain)
Reservé (re-surv-ay)	I reserved / booked

cooperación (cope-air-ass-ee-on / cope-air-ath-ee-on)	cooperation
Cooperé (cope-air-ay)	I cooperated
imaginación (im-a-hin-ass-ee-on / im-a-hin-ath-ee-on)	imagination
Imaginó (im-a-hin-ay)	I imagined
manipulación (man-ip-ool-ass-ee-on / man-ip-ool-ath-ee-on)	manipulation
Manipulé (man-ip-ool-ay)	I manipulated
continuación (con-tin-oo-ass-ee-on / con-tin-oo-ath-ee-on)	continuation
Continué (con-tin-oo-ay)	I continued
participación (par-tis-ip-ass-ee-on / par-tith-ip-ath-ee-on)	participation
Participé (par-tis-ip-ay / par-tith-ip-ay)	I participated
exageración (ex-a-hair-ass-ee-on / ex-a-hair-ath-ee-on)	exaggeration
Exageré (ex-a-hair-ay)	I exaggerated
admiración (ad-mi-rass-ee-on / ad-mi-rath-ee-on)	admiration
Admiré (ad-mi-ray)	I admired
irritación (ee-ri-tass-ee-on / ee-ri-tath-oo-on)	irritation
Irrité (ee-ri-tay)	I irritated
conversación (con-vair-sass-ee-on / con-vair-sath-ee-on)	conversation
Conversé (con-vair-say)	I conversed
Ordené (or-den-ay)	I ordered (preferred in Latin American)
Pedí (pe-dee)	I ordered (literally "I asked for") – (preferred in Spain)
Pagué (pag-ay)	I paid
Hice (ee-say / ee-thay)	I did
la cuenta (la kwen-ta)	the bill

la cena (la say-ner / thay-ner)	the dinner
sopa (soap-er)	soup
una mesa (oon-er may-ser)	a table
una habitación (oon-er ab-it-ass-ee-on / ab-it-ath-ee-on)	a room
un taxi (oon taxi)	a taxi
Preparé la cena. (pre-par-ay la say-ner / thay-ner)	I prepared the dinner.
Ordené sopa para la cena. (or-den-ay soap-er pa-ra la say-ner / thay-ner)	I ordered soup for dinner. (preferred in Latin American)
Pedí sopa para la cena. (pe-dee soap-er pa-ra la say-ner / thay-ner)	I ordered soup for dinner. (preferred in Spain)
Reservé una mesa para usted. (re-surv-ay oon-er may-ser pa-ra oo-stedd)	I booked a table for you.
Ella reservó (ay-a re-surv-o)	She booked / reserved
Ella reservó una mesa para esta noche. (ay-a re-surv-ay oon-er may-ser pa-ra es-ta noch-ay)	She booked / reserved a table for this evening.
Él reservó (el re-surv-o)	He booked / reserved
Él reservó una habitación para dos personas. (el re-surv-o oon-er ab-it-ass-ee-on / ab-it-ath-ee-on pa-ra doss pair-so-nass)	He booked / reserved a room for two people.
¿Qué? (kay)	What?
¿Qué preparó? (kay pre-par-o)	What did you prepare?
¿Qué preparó usted? (kay pre-par-o oo-sted)	What did you prepare?
¿Qué hizo usted? (kay ee-soe / ee-thoe oo-sted)	What did you do?
Reservé una mesa, ordené la cena y luego pagué la cuenta. ¿Qué hizo usted? (re-surv-ay oon-er may-ser, or-den-ay la say-ner / thay-ner ee loo-way-go pag-ay la kwen-ta. kay ee-soe / ee-thoe oo-sted)	I booked a table, ordered dinner and then paid the bill. What did you do?

Tengo la intención de… (ten-go la in-ten-see-on / in-ten-thee-on dey)	I'm planning to… (literally "I have the intention of…")
Tengo la intención de volver a España en mayo. (ten-go la in-ten-see-on / in-ten-thee-on dey vol-vair a es-pan-ya en my-oh)	I'm planning to go back to Spain in May.
Tengo miedo de… (ten-go mee-ed-oh dey)	I'm scared of… (literally "I have fear of…")
Tengo miedo de volver a España en septiembre. (ten-go mee-ed-oh dey vol-vair a es-pan-ya en sep-tee-em-brey)	I'm scared of going back to Spain in September.
¿De verdad? (dey vair-dad)	Really?
por lo que (poor-low-kay)	so
pero (pair-o)	but
Tengo ganas de… (ten-go ga-nas dey)	I feel like… / I fancy… (literally "I have desire of…")
Sí, tengo ganas de volver a Barcelona, pero tengo miedo de volar, por lo que tengo la intención de tomar el Eurostar. (see ten-go ga-nas dey vol-vair a bar-sair-loan-er / bar-thair-loan er pair-o ten-go mee-ed-oh dey vol-ar, poor-low-kay ten-go la in-ten-see-on / in-ten-thee-on dey to-mar el e-oo-roe-star)	Yes, I feel like going back to Barcelona but I'm scared of flying, so I'm planning to take the Eurostar.
Tengo ganas de comprar algo esta mañana. (ten-go ga-nas dey com-prar al-go es-ta man-yarn-a)	I feel like / fancy buying something this morning.
Tengo ganas de leer algo esta tarde. (ten-go ga-nas dey lay-air al-go es-ta tar-dey)	I feel like / fancy reading something this afternoon.
Tiene (tee-en-ey)	You have (formal)
Tiene ganas de comer algo esta noche. (tee-en-ey ga-nas dey kom-air al-go es-ta noch-ay)	You feel like eating something this evening. (formal)

Necesito (ness-e-seet-oh / neth-e-seet-oh)	I need
Necesito hablar español. (ness-e-seet-oh / neth-e-seet-oh a-blar es-pa-nyol)	I need to speak Spanish.
Necesito un taxi. (ness-e-seet-oh / neth-e-seet-oh oon taxi)	I need a taxi.
Necesito una habitación. (ness-e-seet-oh / neth-e-seet-oh oon-er ab-it-ass-ee-on / ab-it-ath-ee-on)	I need a room.
Necesito ayuda. (ness-e-seet-oh / neth-e-seet-oh a-yoo-der)	I need help.
¡Necesitas ayuda, camarada! (ness-e-seet-ass / neth-e-seet-ass a-yoo-der ca-ma-ra-da)	You need help, mate!
Odio (oh-dee-oh)	I hate
¡Odio volar! (oh-dee-oh vol-ar)	I hate flying!
Odio vivir con mis suegros. (odio viv-eer kon miss soo-egg-ros)	I hate living with my in-laws.
Odias comer con mis padres. (oh-dee-ass sey-nan-doh kon miss pard-res)	You hate having dinner with my parents. (informal)
Odia trabajar aquí. (oh-dee-a trab-a-har a-key)	You hate working here. (formal)
Estaba (es-tah-bah)	I was
solitario (so-lit-ar-ee-oh)	solitary
contrario (kon-trar-ee-oh)	contrary
ordinario (or-din-ar-ee-oh)	ordinary
Estaba a punto de… (es-tah-bah a poon-toe dey)	I was about to… / I was just about to… (literally "I was at point of…")
Estaba a punto de preparar la cena. (es-tah-bah a poon-toe dey pre-par-ar la say-ner / thay-ner)	I was about to prepare the dinner / I was just about to prepare the dinner.

Estaba a punto de pagar la cuenta. (es-tah-bah a poon-toe dey pag-ar la kwen-ta)	I was about to pay the bill.
Estaba a punto de reservar una mesa. (es-tah-bah a poon-toe dey re-surv-ar oon-er may-ser)	I was just about to book a table.
Me llamaste. (may yah-mah-stay)	You called me / You did call me / You have called me. (informal)
cuando (kwan-doh)	when
Estaba a punto de reservar un taxi cuando me llamaste. (es-tah-bah a poon-toe dey re-surv-ar oon taxi kwan-doh may yah-mah-stay.)	I was just about to book a taxi when you called me.
Estaba a punto de salir cuando sonó el teléfono. (es-tah-bah a poon-toe dey sal-ear kwan-doh sonn-oh el tel-ef-on-oh)	I was about to leave when the telephone rang.
Estaba a punto de telefonearte cuando tocaste a la puerta. (es-tah-bah a poon-toe dey tel-ef-own-ay-ar-tay kwan-doh toe-kas-tey a la pwer-ta)	I was just about to phone you when you knocked at the door. (informal)
Estaba a punto de reservar un taxi cuando comenzó a llover. (es-tah-bah a poon-toe dey re-surv-ar oon taxi kwan-doh emp-ess-oh / emp-eth-oh a yove-air)	I was just about to order a taxi when it started to rain.
Llegaste. (ye-gah-stay)	You have arrived / You arrived / You did arrive. (informal)
Lo siento. (lo see-en-toe)	I'm sorry.
un poco (oon pock-oh)	a little / a bit
Estaba un poco distraído / distraída. (es-tah-bah oon pock-oh dis-tray-doh / dis-tray-da)	I was a little preoccupied / distracted.

Estaba ocupado / ocupada... (es-tah-bah occ-oopa-doh / occ-oopa-da)	I was busy...
Lo siento, estaba ocupado / ocupada cenando cuando llegaste. (lo see-en-toe, es-tah-bah occ-oopa-doh / occ-oopa-da sey-nan-doh kwan-doh ye-gah-stay)	I'm sorry, I was busy having dinner when you arrived. (informal)
Lo siento, estaba ocupado / ocupada preparando la cena cuando llegaste, por lo que estaba un poco distraído / distraída. (lo see-en-toe, es-tah-bah occ-oopa-doh / occ-oopa-da pre-par-ar la say-ner / thay-ner kwan-doh ye-gah-stay poor-low-kee es-tah-bah oon pock-oh dis-tray-doh / dis-tray-da)	I'm sorry, I was busy preparing the dinner when you arrived, so I was a bit distracted. (informal)
Estaba ocupado / ocupada ordenando la casa cuando llegó mi madre. (es-tah-bah occ-oopa-doh / occ-oopa-da or-de-nan-doh la ca-sa kwan-doh yeg-oh mee mar-dray)	I was busy tidying the house when my mother arrived.
Estaba ocupado / ocupada pintando cuando me llamaste. (es-tah-bah occ-oopa-doh / occ-oopa-da peen-tan-doh kwan-doh may yah-mah-stay)	I was busy painting when you called me.
Estaba ocupado / ocupada hablando por teléfono cuando llegó tu carta. (es-tah-bah occ-oopa-doh / occ-oopa-da ah-blan-doh por te-ley-foh-noh kwan-doh yeg-oh too car-ta)	I was busy speaking on the telephone when your letter arrived.
julio (hoo-lee-oh)	July
en julio (en hoo-lee-oh)	in July

Visité Barcelona en julio. (visit-ay bar-sair-loan-er / bar-thair-loan-er en hoo-lee-oh)	I visited Barcelona in July.
Tengo la intención de visitar Barcelona en julio. (ten-go la in-ten-see-on / in-ten-thee-on dey visit-ar bar-sair-loan-er / bar-thair-loan-er)	I'm planning to visit Barcelona in July.
Voy (voy a)	I'm going
Voy a España en septiembre. (voy a es-pan-ya en sep-tee-em-brey)	I'm going to Spain in September.
por... (por)	because of...
por usted (por oo-sted)	because of you (formal)
por ti (por tee)	because of you (informal)
gracias a... (gra-see-ass a)	thanks to...
¡Gracias a mí! (gra-see-ass a mee)	Thanks to me!
¡Voy a España en julio por ti! (voy a es-pan-ya en hoo-lee-oh por tee)	I'm going to Spain in July because of you! (informal)
¿Quieres? (kee-air-es)	Do you want? (literally "want you?") – (informal)
¿Quieres preparar la cena esta noche? (kee-air-es pre-par-ar la say-ner / thay-ner es-ta noch-ay)	Do you want to prepare the dinner this evening? (informal)
¿Quieres comer algo? (kee-air-es sey-nan-doh al-go)	Do you want to eat something? (informal)
Quieres (kee-air-es)	You want (informal)
decir (de-seer / de-theer)	to say
Quieres decir (kee-air-es de-seer / de-theer)	You mean (literally "you want to say") – (informal)
¡Voy a España en julio por ti! (voy a es-pan-ya en hoo-lee-oh por tee)	I'm going to Spain in July because of you! (informal)
¿Por mí? ¡Quieres decir "gracias a mí"! (por mee kee-air-es de-seer / de-theer gra-see-ass a mee)	Because of me? You mean thanks to me! (informal)

En realidad, voy a Madrid también. (en ray-al-ee-dad, voy a ma-drid tam-bee-en)	Actually, I'm going to Madrid too.
En realidad, voy a España el mes que viene. (en ray-al-ee-dad, voy a es-pan-ya el mess kay vee-enn-ey)	Actually, I'm going to Spain next month.
En realidad, voy a Barcelona el año que viene. (en ray-al-ee-dad, voy a bar-sair-loan-er / bar-thair-loan-er el an-yoh kay vee-enn-ey)	Actually, I'm going to Barcelona next year.
un billete (oon bee-yet-ey)	a ticket
uy (oy)	wow
gracias (gra-see-ass)	thanks
¡Vamos entonces! (var-mos en-ton-sess / en-ton-thess)	Let's go!
¡Pero el Eurostar es excelente! – y estaba a punto de reservar un billete cuando llegaste. (pair-o el e-oo-roe-star es ex-se-lent-ey / ex-the-lent-ey ee es-tah-bah a poon-toe dey re-surv-ar oon bee-yet-ey kwan-doh ye-gah-stay)	But the Eurostar is excellent! – and I was just about to book a ticket when you arrived.
Ay, lo siento. En realidad, tengo ganas de visitar Barcelona también. (eye lo see-en-toe. en ray-al-ee-dad ten-go ga-nas dey visit-ar bar-sair-loan-er / bar-thair-loan-er tam-bee-en)	Oh, sorry. Actually, I feel like visiting Barcelona too.
Sí, cuando hablas de Barcelona suenas tan entusiasmado. (see, kwan-doh ab-lass dey bar-sair-loan-er / bar-thair-loan-er swen-ass tan en-tooz-ee-as-mard-oh)	Yes, when you talk about Barcelona, you sound so enthusiastic.
¡Uy, gracias! ¡Vamos entonces! (oy gra-see-ass. var-mos en-ton-sess / en-ton-thess)	Wow, thanks! Let's go then!

Having worked your way through the Spanish-to-English list above without making any mistakes, you will now want to get to the point where you can also work through the English-to-Spanish list below without making any mistakes. You should feel free to do this over multiple days or even weeks if you feel you need to. Just take your time and work at it until constructing the sentences and recalling the words become second nature to you.

the weekend	**el fin de semana** (el fin dey sem-arn-er)
romantic	**romántico** (roe-man-tick-oh)
typical	**típico** (tip-ick-oh)
political	**político** (po-li-tick-oh)
logical	**lógico** (lo-hee-koh)
historical	**histórico** (ee-sto-rick-oh)
critical	**crítico** (kri-tick-oh)
classical	**clásico** (clas-ick-oh)
electrical	**eléctrico** (el-ek-trick-oh)
identical	**idéntico** (ee-dent-ick-oh)
biological	**biológico** (bee-oh-lo-hee-koh)
enthusiastic	**entusiasmado** (en-tooz-ee-as-mard-oh)
I visited	**Visité** (visit-ay)
Barcelona	**Barcelona** (bar-sair-loan-er / bar-thair-loan-er)
Madrid	**Madrid** (ma-drid)
I visited Madrid.	**Visité Madrid.** (visit-ay ma-drid)
I spent	**Pasé** (pass-ay)
You spent	**Pasó** (pass-o)
We spent	**Pasamos** (pass-arm-oss)
September	**septiembre** (sep-tee-em-brey)
Christmas (literally "the Christmas")	**la Navidad** (la na-vee-dad)
in Barcelona	**en Barcelona** (en bar-sair-loan-er / bar-thair-loan-er)

in Spain	en España (en es-pan-ya)
in Mexico	en México (en me-hee-koe)
We spent Christmas in Mexico.	Pasamos la Navidad en México. (pass-arm-oss la na-vee-dad en me-hee-koe)
You spent September in Spain.	Pasó septiembre en España. (pass-o sep-tee-em-brey en es-pan-ya)
and	y (ee)
it was	fue (fway)
it was romantic	fue romántico (fway roe-man-tick-oh)
lovely / adorable	adorable (ad-or-arb-lay)
it was lovely / it was adorable	fue adorable (fway ad-or-arb-lay)
I spent the weekend in Barcelona… and it was lovely.	Pasé el fin de semana en Barcelona… y fue adorable. (pass-ay el fin dey sem-arn-er en bar-sair-loan-er / bar-thair-loan-er ee fway ad-or-arb-lay)
invitation	invitación (in-vit-ass-ee-on)
I invited	Invité (in-vit-ay)
preparation	preparación (pray-par-ass-ee-on)
I prepared	Preparé (pre-par-ay)
reservation (preferred in Latin American)	reservación (re-surv-ass-ee-on / re-surv-ath-ee-on)
reservation (preferred in Spain)	reserva (re-surv-a)
I reserved / booked	Reservé (re-surv-ay)
cooperation	cooperación (cope-air-ass-ee-on / cope-air-ath-ee-on)
I cooperated	Cooperé (cope-air-ay)
imagination	imaginación (im-a-hin-ass-ee-on / im-a-hin-ath-ee-on)
I imagined	Imaginé (im-a-hin-ay)
manipulation	manipulación (man-ip-ool-ass-ee-on / man-ip-ool-ath-ee-on)
I manipulated	Manipulé (man-ip-ool-ay)

continuation	**continuación** (con-tin-oo-ass-ee-on / con-tin-oo-ath-ee-on)
I continued	**Continué** (con-tin-oo-ay)
participation	**participación** (par-tis-ip-ass-ee-on / par-tith-ip-ath-ee-on)
I participated	**Participé** (par-tis-ip-ay / par-tith-ip-ay)
exaggeration	**exageración** (ex-a-hair-ass-ee-on / ex-a-hair-ath-ee-on)
I exaggerated	**Exageré** (ex-a-hair-ay)
admiration	**admiración** (ad-mi-rass-ee-on / ad-mi-rath-ee-on)
I admired	**Admiré** (ad-mi-ray)
irritation	**irritación** (ee-ri-tass-ee-on / ee-ri-tath-ee-on)
I irritated	**Irrité** (ee-ri-tay)
conversation	**conversación** (con-vair-sass-ee-on / con-vair-sath-ee-on)
I conversed	**Conversé** (con-vair-say)
I ordered (preferred in Latin American)	**Ordené** (or-den-ay)
I ordered (literally "I asked for") – (preferred in Spain)	**Pedí** (pe-dee)
I paid	**Pagué** (pag-ay)
I did	**Hice** (ee-say / ee-thay)
the bill	**la cuenta** (la kwen-ta)
the dinner	**la cena** (la say-ner / thay-ner)
soup	**sopa** (soap-er)
a table	**una mesa** (oon-er may-ser)
a room	**una habitación** (oon-er ab-it-ass-ee-on / ab-it-ath-ee-on)
a taxi	**un taxi** (oon taxi)
I prepared the dinner.	**Preparé la cena.** (pre-par-ay la say-ner / thay-ner)

I ordered soup for dinner. (preferred in Latin American)	Ordené sopa para la cena. (or-den-ay soap-er pa-ra la say-ner / thay-ner)
I ordered soup for dinner. (preferred in Spain)	Pedí sopa para la cena. (pe-dee soap-er pa-ra la say-ner / thay-ner)
I booked a table for you.	Reservé una mesa para usted. (re-surv-ay oon-er may-ser pa-ra oo-stedd)
She booked / reserved	Ella reservó (ay-a re-surv-o)
She booked / reserved a table for this evening.	Ella reservó una mesa para esta noche. (ay-a re-surv-ay oon-er may-ser pa-ra es-ta noch-ay)
He booked / reserved	Él reservó (el re-surv-o)
He booked / reserved a room for two people.	Él reservó una habitación para dos personas. (el re-surv-o oon-er ab-it-ass-ee-on / ab-it-ath-ee-on pa-ra doss pair-so-nass)
What?	¿Qué? (kay)
What did you prepare?	¿Qué preparó? (kay pre-par-o)
What did you prepare?	¿Qué preparó usted? (kay pre-par-o oo-sted)
What did you do?	¿Qué hizo usted? (kay ee-soe / ee-thoe oo-sted)
I booked a table, ordered dinner and then paid the bill. What did you do?	Reservé una mesa, ordené la cena y luego pagué la cuenta. ¿Qué hizo usted? (re-surv-ay oon-er may-ser, or-den-ay la say-ner / thay-ner ee loo-way-go pag-ay la kwen-ta. kay ee-soe / ee-thoe oo-sted)
I'm planning to… (literally "I have the intention of…")	Tengo la intención de… (ten-go la in-ten-see-on / in-ten-thee-on dey)
I'm planning to go back to Spain in May.	Tengo la intención de volver a España en mayo. (ten-go la in-ten-see-on / in-ten-thee-on dey vol-vair a es-pan-ya en my-oh)
I'm scared of… (literally "I have fear of…")	Tengo miedo de… (ten-go mee-ed-oh dey)

I'm scared of going back to Spain in September.	Tengo miedo de volver a España en septiembre. (ten-go mee-ed-oh dey vol-vair a es-pan-ya en sep-tee-em-brey)
Really?	¿De verdad? (dey vair-dad)
so	por lo que (poor low kay)
but	pero (pair-o)
I feel like… / I fancy… (literally "I have desire of…")	Tengo ganas de… (ten-go ga-nas dey)
Yes, I feel like going back to Barcelona but I'm scared of flying, so I'm planning to take the Eurostar.	Sí, tengo ganas de volver a Barcelona, pero tengo miedo de volar, por lo que tengo la intención de tomar el Eurostar. (see ten-go ga-nas dey vol-vair a bar-sair-loan-er / bar-thair-loan-er pair-o ten-go mee-ed-oh dey vol-ar, poor-low-kay ten-go la in-ten-see-on / in-ten-thee-on dey to-mar el e-oo-roe-star)
I feel like / fancy buying something this morning.	Tengo ganas de comprar algo esta mañana. (ten-go ga-nas dey com-prar al-go es-ta man-yarn-a)
I feel like / fancy reading something this afternoon.	Tengo ganas de leer algo esta tarde. (ten-go ga-nas dey lay-air al-go es-ta tar-dey)
You have (formal)	Tiene (tee-en-ey)
You feel like eating something this evening. (formal)	Tiene ganas de comer algo esta noche. (tee-en-ey ga-nas dey kom-air al-go es-ta noch-ay)
I need	Necesito (ness-e-seet-oh / neth-e-seet-oh)
I need to speak Spanish.	Necesito hablar español. (ness-e-seet-oh / neth-e-seet-oh a-blar es-pa-nyol)
I need a taxi.	Necesito un taxi. (ness-e-seet-oh / neth-e-seet-oh oon taxi)

I need a room.	Necesito una habitación. (ness-e-seet-oh / neth-e-seet-oh oon-er ab-it-ass-ee-on / ab-it-ath-ee-on)
I need help.	Necesito ayuda. (ness-e-seet-oh / neth-e-seet-oh a-yoo-der)
You need help, mate!	¡Necesitas ayuda, camarada! (ness-e-seet-ass / neth-e-seet-ass a-yoo-der ca-ma-ra-da)
I hate	Odio (oh-dee-oh)
I hate flying!	¡Odio volar! (oh-dee-oh vol-ar)
I hate living with my in-laws.	Odio vivir con mis suegros. (odio viv-eer kon miss soo-egg-ros)
You hate having dinner with my parents. (informal)	Odias comer con mis padres. (oh-dee-ass sey-nan-doh kon miss pard-res)
You hate working here. (formal)	Odia trabajar aquí. (oh-dee-a trab-a-har a-key)
I was	Estaba (es-tah-bah)
solitary	solitario (so-lit-ar-ee-oh)
contrary	contrario (kon-trar-ee-oh)
ordinary	ordinario (or-din-ar-ee-oh)
I was about to… / I was just about to… (literally "I was at point of…")	Estaba a punto de… (es-tah-bah a poon-toe dey)
I was about to prepare the dinner / I was just about to prepare the dinner.	Estaba a punto de preparar la cena. (es-tah-bah a poon-toe dey pre-par-ar la say-ner / thay-ner)
I was about to pay the bill.	Estaba a punto de pagar la cuenta. (es-tah-bah a poon-toe dey pag-ar la kwen-ta)
I was just about to book a table.	Estaba a punto de reservar una mesa. (es-tah-bah a poon-toe dey re-surv-ar oon-er may-ser)
You called me / You did call me / You have called me. (informal)	Me llamaste. (may yah-mah-stay)

when	cuando (kwan-doh)
I was just about to book a taxi when you called me.	Estaba a punto de reservar un taxi cuando me llamaste. (es-tah-bah a poon-toe dey re-surv-ar oon taxi kwan-doh may yah-mah-stay.)
I was about to leave when the telephone rang.	Estaba a punto de salir cuando sonó el teléfono. (es-tah-bah a poon-toe dey sal-ear kwan-doh sonn-oh el tel-ef-on-oh)
I was just about to phone you when you knocked at the door. (informal)	Estaba a punto de telefonearte cuando tocaste a la puerta. (es-tah-bah a poon-toe dey tel-ef-own-ay-ar-tay kwan-doh toe-kas-tey a la pwer-ta)
I was just about to order a taxi when it started to rain.	Estaba a punto de reservar un taxi cuando comenzó a llover. (es-tah-bah a poon-toe dey re-surv-ar oon taxi kwan-doh emp-ess-oh / emp-eth-oh a yove-air)
You have arrived / You arrived / You did arrive. (informal)	Llegaste. (ye-gah-stay)
I'm sorry.	Lo siento. (lo see-en-toe)
a little / a bit	un poco (oon pock-oh)
I was a little preoccupied / distracted.	Estaba un poco distraído / distraída. (es-tah-bah oon pock-oh dis-tray-doh / dis-tray-da)
I was busy…	Estaba ocupado / ocupada… (es-tah-bah occ-oopa-doh / occ-oopa-da)
I'm sorry, I was busy having dinner when you arrived. (informal)	Lo siento, estaba ocupado / ocupada cenando cuando llegaste. (lo see-en-toe, es-tah-bah occ-oopa-doh / occ-oopa-da sey-nan-doh kwan-doh ye-gah-stay)

I'm sorry, I was busy preparing the dinner when you arrived, so I was a bit distracted. (informal)	Lo siento, estaba ocupado / ocupada preparando la cena cuando llegaste, por lo que estaba un poco distraído / distraída. (lo see-en-toe, es-tah-bah occ-oopa-doh / occ-oopa-da pre-par-ar la say-ner / thay-ner kwan-doh ye-gah-stay poor-low-kee es-tah-bah oon pock-oh dis-tray-doh / dis-tray-da)
I was busy tidying the house when my mother arrived.	Estaba ocupado / ocupada ordenando la casa cuando llegó mi madre. (es-tah-bah occ-oopa-doh / occ-oopa-da or-de-nan-doh la ca-sa kwan-doh yeg-oh mee mar-dray)
I was busy painting when you called me.	Estaba ocupado / ocupada pintando cuando me llamaste. (es-tah-bah occ-oopa-doh / occ-oopa-da peen-tan-doh kwan-doh may yah-mah-stay)
I was busy speaking on the telephone when your letter arrived.	Estaba ocupado / ocupada hablando por teléfono cuando llegó tu carta. (es-tah-bah occ-oopa-doh / occ-oopa-da ah-blan-doh por te-ley-foh-noh kwan-doh yeg-oh too car-ta)
July	julio (hoo-lee-oh)
in July	en julio (en hoo-lee-oh)
I visited Barcelona in July.	Visité Barcelona en julio. (visit-ay bar-sair-loan-er / bar-thair-loan-er en hoo-lee-oh)
I'm planning to visit Barcelona in July.	Tengo la intención de visitar Barcelona en julio. (ten-go la in-ten-see-on / in-ten-thee-on dey visit-ar bar-sair-loan-er / bar-thair-loan-er)
I'm going	Voy (voy a)
I'm going to Spain in September.	Voy a España en septiembre. (voy a es-pan-ya en sep-tee-em-brey)
because of…	por… (por)

because of you (formal)	por usted (por oo-sted)
because of you (informal)	por ti (por tee)
thanks to...	gracias a... (gra-see-ass a)
Thanks to me!	¡Gracias a mí! (gra-see-ass a mee)
I'm going to Spain in July because of you! (informal)	¡Voy a España en julio por ti! (voy a es-pan-ya en hoo-lee-oh por tee)
Do you want? (literally "want you?") – (informal)	¿Quieres? (kee-air-es)
Do you want to prepare the dinner this evening? (informal)	¿Quieres preparar la cena esta noche? (kee-air-es pre-par-ar la say-ner / thay-ner es-ta noch-ay)
Do you want to eat something? (informal)	¿Quieres comer algo? (kee-air-es sey-nan-doh al-go)
You want (informal)	Quieres (kee-air-es)
to say	decir (de-seer / de-theer)
You mean (literally "you want to say") – (informal)	Quieres decir (kee-air-es de-seer / de-theer)
I'm going to Spain in July because of you! (informal)	¡Voy a España en julio por ti! (voy a es-pan-ya en hoo-lee-oh por tee)
Because of me? You mean thanks to me! (informal)	¿Por mí? ¡Quieres decir "gracias a mí"! (por mee kee-air-es de-seer / de-theer gra-see-ass a mee)
Actually, I'm going to Madrid too.	En realidad, voy a Madrid también. (en ray-al-ee-dad, voy a ma-drid tam-bee-en)
Actually, I'm going to Spain next month.	En realidad, voy a España el mes que viene. (en ray-al-ee-dad, voy a es-pan-ya el mess kay vee-enn-ey)
Actually, I'm going to Barcelona next year.	En realidad, voy a Barcelona el año que viene. (en ray-al-ee-dad, voy a bar-sair-loan-er / bar-thair-loan-er el an-yoh kay vee-enn-ey)
a ticket	un billete (oon bee-yet-ey)
wow	uy (oy)
thanks	gracias (gra-see-ass)

Let's go!	¡Vamos entonces! (var-mos en-ton-sess / en-ton-thess)
But the Eurostar is excellent! – and I was just about to book a ticket when you arrived.	¡Pero el Eurostar es excelente! – y estaba a punto de reservar un billete cuando llegaste. (pair-o el e-oo-roe-star es ex-se-lent-ey / ex-the-lent-ey ee es-tah-bah a poon-toe dey re-surv-ar oon bee-yet-ey kwan-doh ye-gah-stay)
Oh, sorry. Actually, I feel like visiting Barcelona too.	Ay, lo siento. En realidad, tengo ganas de visitar Barcelona también. (eye lo see-en-toe. en ray-al-ee-dad ten-go ga-nas dey visit-ar bar-sair-loan-er / bar-thair-loan-er tam-bee-en)
Yes, when you talk about Barcelona, you sound so enthusiastic.	Sí, cuando hablas de Barcelona suenas tan entusiasmado. (see, kwan-doh ab-lass dey bar-sair-loan-er / bar-thair-loan-er swen-ass tan en-tooz-ee-as-mard-oh)
Wow, thanks! Let's go then!	¡Uy, gracias! ¡Vamos entonces! (oy gra-see-ass. var-mos en-ton-sess / en-ton-thess)

If you've got through this without making any mistakes, then you're ready to read the final Between Chapters Tip, which will tell you what to do next.

Well done for getting this far! Well done indeed...

Between Chapters Tip!

What to do next

Well, here you are at the end of the final chapter. You have worked hard and yet a different journey now lies ahead of you!

The questions you should be asking, of course, are: "what is that journey exactly?" and "where do I go from here?"

Where do you go first?

Well, that will depend to some degree on what you already knew when you began working through this book.

If you have found this book useful, then I would recommend moving on to my audio course entitled "Learn Spanish with Paul Noble". It uses the same method as this book except that you listen to it rather than read it. It will help to develop your understanding of how to structure Spanish sentences and how to use Spanish tenses, while at the same time gently expanding your vocabulary further still. In addition to that, the course will teach you plenty of tricks that will allow you to make rapid progress.

And after that?

Once you have completed the audio course, I then recommend that you use what I have at different times called "The Frasier Method", "The Game of Thrones Method", "The Buffy the Vampire Slayer Method" and "The Friends Method" – but the name isn't too important.

What is important is how the method works, which is like this...

Once you have gained a functional vocabulary and understanding of structures and tenses (from having used both this book and my audio course), I recommend that you then purchase an English language television series – a long one. It should ideally have something like 50 episodes or more (100 is even better). And it should be something that you have watched previously.

This might seem an odd way to learn Spanish but it's not. Trust me. It is in fact a very easy and enjoyable way to develop your ability in the language. Now listen well because I'm going to explain to you exactly how this method works.

Almost all major, successful, long-running English language TV series will be available with a Spanish dub. Typically, the version you can buy locally will have the ability to switch the language to Spanish, if not you can go to eBay or Amazon Spain and order the Spanish dubbed version from there.

Now, what you're going to do with the series you've chosen is to watch it in Spanish. You should watch one episode at a time, whenever it's convenient for you to do so. And, when you watch it, you're not only going to watch it dubbed into Spanish but you're also going to put on the Spanish subtitles. If you use the English subtitles, you will spend your whole time reading them and will learn nothing.

Now while you watch the Spanish dub of the series you've chosen, I want you to keep a pen and notepad handy and, when you hear a word you're not familiar with, I want you to write it down. Do this with the first twenty words you don't recognise. Once you've written those twenty down, don't bother writing any more for the rest of the episode. Instead, all I want you to do is to put a tick beside each of those words every time you hear them during the rest of the episode.

When the episode is finished, take a look at how many ticks each word has. Any word with more than three ticks beside it is something you need to learn. So, look it up in a dictionary and then write the English word beside it in your notepad. Once you have a translation for each, use the checklist technique from this book to go through them until you can remember roughly what each word means. Then let yourself forget about them.

The following day, repeat this whole process again during the next episode. Something you'll begin to notice very quickly, however, is that the words that came up a lot in the first episode will also come up a lot in the second. This is because, on the one hand, any words that came up a lot the first day are likely to be quite important words anyway and, on the other, because you're watching a TV series, the same themes are typically repeated in different episodes. So, if you like *Game of Thrones*, you're going to very quickly learn the words for things such as "castle", "horse" and "wench". If you like *Friends*, then you're going to very quickly learn the words for things like "coffee shop", "girlfriend" and "breakup".

And it's precisely because these same themes and the same language come up again and again that watching a long series becomes much more valuable than simply watching something like Spanish films, for example. Were you to watch Spanish films instead, you would quickly find that each film would almost certainly have a different theme and therefore the vocabulary would not repeat itself so much. When you watch a TV series, however, because you're looking up the most important vocabulary and because it's repeated in the series again and again and again, you really do end up remembering it. It becomes extremely familiar to you.

Now, you may say to this "Okay, fair enough, but why does it have to be an English language series dubbed into Spanish rather than simply a Spanish one? And why should it be something I've seen before in English, why not something totally new?" The reason for this is simple: you will learn far more, far more quickly doing it this way. And why? Well, because if you decide to watch a Spanish TV series, instead of an English one, you will immediately encounter unfamiliar cultural issues – the way people live, where they do their shopping, what they cook – much of this will be different. This therefore means that, if you watch a Spanish series, you will not only be trying to figure out what something means linguistically but, also very frequently, what something means culturally. It will simply present another set of barriers to understanding, which is why it's best to begin with something familiar.

This leads us on to why it should be a series that you've already watched in English. For exactly the same reasons given a moment ago, you should also try to choose a TV series you've watched before because you will already be familiar with the context of the story. This will make it far easier to grasp what is being said, to catch words, to get the jokes and to increase your understanding more rapidly. Often, you will find that you can actually guess what a particular word means because you are already familiar with the context and this will make it far easier to pick up that word in Spanish.

So, once you're finished with this book and my audio course (you will need to have done both to be ready to use this "Game of Thrones Method"), go and watch a TV series and keep a pen and notepad handy and use it in exactly the way I've described above.

If you do this, both you and your Spanish will soar!

Good Luck! - ¡Buena Suerte!

PRONUNCIATION GUIDE

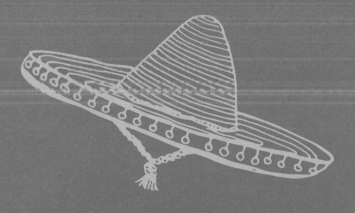

Guide to the pronunciation of individual letters

In case you're struggling with any of the trickier Spanish words and sounds, I'm providing you with an additional resource below, which should make pronouncing even the most peculiar-sounding Spanish words easy peasy.

Forvo

One wonderful resource that should help you with the pronunciation of more or less any Spanish word is Forvo.

Forvo is a free service, which also requires no membership and no logins, where thousands of native speaker volunteers have recorded themselves saying various words from their languages.

So, if you're not sure whether you've got the pronunciation of a word quite right and it's worrying you, then simply go to forvo.com and type in that word. Frequently, you will find that the word has been recorded by several different people and so you can listen to multiple examples of the word until you feel confident that you know how to pronounce it.

So, if in doubt, go to forvo.com and have a listen!

A guide to pronunciation is provided under every word and sentence in this book. However, if you want some additional guidance on how to pronounce the trickier sounds in Spanish, you will find below some help regarding how to pronounce Spanish words when you see them written down.

Just take a look at the letters below to find how they are typically pronounced in Spanish:

j is pronounced like the English letter "h" at the beginning of the words "hat" and "hot".

g before an "i" or "e" is also pronounced like the English letter "h" at the beginning of the words "hat" and "hot".

g before an "a", "o" or "u", however, is pronounced like the "g" in the English words "gun" and "game".

h is silent in Spanish.

z is pronounced differently depending on where you are – it is pronounced like the "s" in the English words "sit" and "sand" in Latin America but like the "th" in "think" or "thanks" across most of Spain.

c before an "i" or "e" is also pronounced like the "s" in the English words "sit" and "sand" in Latin America but like the "th" in "think" or "thanks" across most of Spain.

c before any letters other than "i" or "e" is pronounced like the "c" in the English words "cup" and "coin".

d is pronounced like the "d" in "dog" or "dirt" except when it comes at the end of a word or between two vowels.

d at the end of a word or between two vowels is pronounced very softly and sounds similar to the "th" in the English word "the".

ñ is pronounced as a "ny" sound, like in the country name "Kenya".

b and **V** are pronounced in exactly the same way as one another in Spanish. They are each pronounced somewhere between an English letter "b" and "v" but are a little softer.

As for the vowels:

a is pronounced like the "a" in "father".

e is pronounced like the "e" in "get".

i is pronounced like the "i" in "machine".

o is pronounced like the "o" in "no".

u is pronounced like the "oo" in "cool".